The Reference Shelf®

U.S. National Debate Topic 2005–2006

U.S. Civil Liberties

Edited by Lara Weibgen

Editorial Advisor Lynn M. Messina

The Reference Shelf
Volume 77 • Number 3

The H. W. Wilson Company
2005

The Reference Shelf

The books in this series contain reprints of articles, excerpts from books, addresses on current issues, and studies of social trends in the United States and other countries. There are six separately bound numbers in each volume, all of which are usually published in the same calendar year. Numbers one through five are each devoted to a single subject, providing background information and discussion from various points of view and concluding with a subject index and comprehensive bibliography that lists books, pamphlets, and abstracts of additional articles on the subject. The final number of each volume is a collection of recent speeches, and it contains a cumulative speaker index. Books in the series may be purchased individually or on subscription.

Library of Congress has cataloged this title as follows:

U.S. national debate topic 2005–2006: U.S. civil liberties / edited by Lara Weibgen
         p. cm—(Reference Shelf; v. 77, no. 3)
     "Editorial Advisor Lynn M. Messina."
     Includes bibliographical references and index.
     ISBN 0-8242-1048-4
     1. Civil rights—United States. I. Title: U.S. civil liberties. II. Title: U.S. national
debate topic 2005–2006. III. Title: United States national debate topic 2005–2006.
IV. Weibgen, Lara. V. Series.
KF4749.A2U14 2005
342.7308'5—dc22

                                                                2005045266

Cover: The forearm and torch of the Statue of Liberty on display at the Centennial Exposition in Philadelphia, 1876. (Photo by FPG/Getty Images)

Visit H.W. Wilson's Web site: www.hwwilson.com

Printed in the United States of America

Contents

Preface

The word *liberty* has long been a mainstay of discussions about U.S. history and identity. Stamped on every U.S. coin, it is uttered daily by schoolchildren taught to sing of their country as a "sweet land of liberty" and recite the Pledge of Allegiance, which promises "liberty and justice for all." It is the name of Philadelphia's famous Liberty Bell, which rang in several landmark events during the colonial period, including the first public reading of the Declaration of Independence. In 1775 Patrick Henry gave memorable voice to American colonists' desire for freedom from British rule when he exclaimed, "Give me liberty or give me death!" Fourteen years later, the framers of the U.S. Constitution wrote of their wish to "secure the Blessings of Liberty to ourselves and our Posterity."

During the 19th century, *liberty* took on new connotations as it became a catchword among antislavery activists. In 1837 the New York Anti-Slavery Society used an image of the Liberty Bell as a frontispiece for a publication titled—what else?—*Liberty*, and a poem about the Bell appeared some time later in an antislavery newsletter called the *Liberator*. During his Gettysburg Address, Abraham Lincoln described the United States as a nation "conceived in liberty." Some two decades later, the Statue of Liberty (officially titled *Liberty Enlightening the World*) was installed in New York Harbor, where it quickly became a symbol of American freedom to immigrants from around the world.

In 1961, during his inaugural address, President John F. Kennedy cited liberty as one of the most important features of American society, proclaiming that the citizens of the United States would "pay any price, bear any burden, meet any hardship, support any friend, oppose any foe, to assure the survival and success of liberty." Yet by the time this speech was delivered, the word *liberty* had already become a source of widespread confusion and disagreement among Americans. More and more, people were coming to realize that the monolithic promise of "liberty and justice for all" did not, in fact, apply equally to all U.S. citizens: Although slavery no longer existed, social, economic, and educational inequalities continued to divide Americans along racial lines. In 1964 Malcolm X appropriated Patrick Henry's famous dictum to protest the disenfranchisement of black Americans in U.S. politics, declaring, "It'll be ballots, or it'll be bullets. It'll be liberty, or it will be death." Reclaimed by people who had never received its full benefits, the word *liberty* became both an indictment of and an expression of hope for the United States. As the Civil War historian Eric Foner once remarked, "Freedom is so often defined by its opposite rather than as an idea."

Recent discussions about liberty in the United States have focused on the relationship between the federal government and individual citizens, and in particular on the implications for civil liberties of security policies implemented by the Bush administration in response to the events of 9/11. It is with these new worries and tensions in mind that the articles in this anthology were assembled. The first section of this book presents an overview of the relationship between personal freedom and national security, weighing the federal government's responsibility to protect its citizens from harm against its obligation to respect their individual rights. Readers are introduced to various arguments surrounding the USA PATRIOT (Uniting and Strengthening America by Providing Appropriate Tools Required to Intercept and Obstruct Terrorism) Act, a controversial piece of legislation whose implications for civil liberties have been hotly debated since its passage in October 2001. The second section addresses the subject of racial profiling, presenting cases both for and against the use of ethnic criteria by government officials in their attempts to find and arrest enemies of the state. The third section, which begins with several accounts of instances in which individuals were detained without charge by the federal government, explores the implications of heightened security measures for those suspected, but not explicitly accused, of wrongful activity. In the fourth section, the focus of the book shifts from the public to the private sphere, raising questions about the extent to which the government should be involved in regulating the morality of its citizens, particularly on the subjects of same-sex marriage and abortion. The fifth and final section of the book discusses government surveillance of civilian activities, outlining the tension between the individual's right to privacy and the government's responsibility to investigate and disclose potential security threats.

A belief in the value and necessity of personal freedom looms large in the American imagination. Yet because definitions of liberty change frequently, no single book, let alone one as short as this, could capture the full range of outlooks that together would constitute a peculiarly American view of the subject. Therefore, in assembling this collection, I have tried to present a balanced sampling of contemporary opinions on civil liberties, offsetting politically moderate articles with essays from both left- and right-wing sources. Taken together, these writings are meant to introduce the reader to a series of complex and interrelated issues, with the expectation and understanding that they will raise more questions than they answer.

In closing, I would like to express my gratitude to the authors and original publishers who gave permission to have their articles reprinted here. I would also like to thank my colleagues Lynn Messina, Sandra Watson, and Jennifer Curry for their kind assistance during the planning stages of this book, as well as Isaac-Davy Aronson, Danielle Frank, Daniel Immerwahr, Sam Means, and Ariana Reines for their advice and support.

Lara Weibgen
June 2005

I. Civil Liberties and Terrorism

Editor's Introduction

When Thomas Jefferson drafted the Declaration of Independence, he cited "Life, Liberty and the pursuit of Happiness" as three of the "unalienable Rights" of all people. It is the government's responsibility, he wrote, "to secure these rights" for its citizens; indeed, safeguarding the rights of individuals was presented as the main reason for governments to exist. But how should legislators and federal agents carry out their duty to defend civil rights and liberties during times of danger, when the public welfare is—or is believed to be—at risk? Is it necessary or appropriate for the federal government to place limitations on citizens' entitlement to "Liberty and the pursuit of Happiness" in the interest of maintaining national security, or does this constitute a violation of the founding principles and spirit of the United States?

In "Enduring Freedoms," from the *Spokesman Review*, Carla K. Johnson presents an outline of the conflicts over civil liberties that have emerged in the United States since the terrorist attacks of September 11, 2001. Placing contemporary events and arguments within the context of U.S. history, she begins with a discussion of the controversies surrounding the USA PATRIOT Act, then proceeds to discuss various examples of conflicts that have arisen over interpretations of the Bill of Rights since its ratification in 1791.

Thomas F. Powers offers a more detailed examination of current debates over civil liberties in "Can We Be Secure and Free?," an article first printed in the *Public Interest*. Presenting a nuanced view of arguments advanced by both those who wish to defend individual rights and those who support stronger security measures, he argues that recent controversies have given rise to a false dichotomy that exaggerates the degree to which these concerns must be mutually exclusive. According to Powers, the debate over civil liberties has created unwarranted suspicion and mistrust on both sides; however, he maintains, the differences remain reconcilable.

In "Better Safe Than Sorry," from the *Weekly Standard*, Amitai Etzioni discusses the provisions of the federal government's recent security measures and the opposition they have faced from various sectors of U.S. society. He argues that it is wrong to approach national defense as a zero-sum game in which civil rights and liberties are placed in direct opposition to new safety procedures. According to Etzioni, a close examination of the Bush Administration's homeland security policies finds that their provisions derive from sound constitutional, legal, and ethical sources. Although some recent security measures raise troubling questions, he writes, many were either long overdue or perfectly appropriate under the circumstances. "When all is said and done," Etzioni writes, "most of the measures that the Bush administration has launched since 9/11 are reasonable and necessary."

In "At War with Liberty," Stephen J. Schulhofer, writing for the *American Prospect*, argues that while the Bush administration has gained public approval for its seemingly tough stance against terrorism by restricting civil liberties in various ways, these restrictions have done very little to address the security needs of the country. He concedes that widespread concern about terrorism justifies certain expansions of power in law enforcement, but he also notes that some of these expansions are ineffective and allow federal agents to investigate "suspicious activities" unrelated to terrorism in an invasive, possibly unconstitutional manner.

Finally, in "Acts of Resistance," from *Harper's Magazine*, Elaine Scarry contends that the PATRIOT Act's main purpose has been "to increase the power of the Justice Department and to decrease the rights of individual persons," thereby resulting in governmental infringements on personal privacy and other freedoms ordinarily assured to individuals living in a democracy. These perceived violations of basic rights, Scarry notes, have prompted 272 communities and four state legislatures to pass resolutions that direct residents, including local police officers, to abstain from assisting federal officers in acts that violate the U.S. Constitution. According to Scarry, such local actions constitute a heartening demonstration of U.S. citizens' power to work against government actions that might otherwise undercut the will of the people.

Enduring Freedoms

By Carla K. Johnson
The Spokesman-Review, July 4, 2003

Freedom lives in the lipsticked faces of cross-dressing male cheerleaders marching in a gay pride parade. It lives in the shouted damnations of a street preacher who makes downtown Spokane his pulpit. It lives in a businesswoman who carries a pistol in her purse to protect herself. It lives in a judge reviewing a search warrant before drug detectives can swing their battering ram against a Spokane front door.

This Fourth of July, one year and 10 months after the 9/11 terrorist attacks, the freedoms of the Bill of Rights endure to protect individuals from government overreaching. Controversial from the start, the first 10 amendments to the Constitution continue to provoke some of the most ferocious controversies of the era.

Take, for example, the USA Patriot Act, which gave the federal government broad new powers to investigate terrorism. The country is facing off against itself: Those charged with protecting the nation hear criticism from those who think our civil liberties are being sacrificed in the war on terrorism.

"I recognize the trauma this country has gone through in September 11, but I'm very concerned that has become the basis upon which we take away the freedoms on which this country is founded. I find that to be of tremendous concern to all citizens."

Those words come not from a liberal pundit, but from King County District Court Judge Robert McBeth, a graduate of Mead High School and Washington state's foremost expert on the Fourth Amendment. McBeth, who considers himself a moderate, educates the state's judges on new case law at conferences and in a quarterly report called "Search and Seizure."

As a judge, he needs to be cautious about expressing opinions. But he exercised his freedom of speech in a recent interview. The Patriot Act, passed by Congress shortly after 9/11, concerns him greatly.

"I think the Patriot Act gives the country far greater power to impact our lives than ever before on a mere accusation without having to prove that accusation in court," he says.

Attorney General John Ashcroft and the U.S. Justice Department maintain the nation's anti-terrorism investigations are constitutional and necessary to protect Americans.

Indeed, even a constitutional scholar and critic of the Patriot Act says the aspect of the law he considers most alarming—the computer-driven, multiagency domestic intelligence capability it authorizes—may not be unconstitutional. Courts have held that Americans have no reasonable expectation of privacy in computer records held by third parties.

"The Fourth Amendment covers the stuff in the rolltop desk," says Christopher Pyle, who teaches constitutional law at Mount Holyoke College in South Hadley, Mass. "It does not cover searches of financial computer records, e-mail, travel documents, and all the rest.

"We now entrust our papers and effects to people outside our homes. The government is now accessing that and forbidding the people who maintain that information from letting us know it's being shared."

Librarians have rebelled against the law by shredding records of who is checking out what books, or, as in Spokane, by stripping off identifying information electronically when patrons return books.

The books someone checks out should not be used to build a profile of a suspected terrorist, Spokane Public Library Director Jan Sanders says.

"If the pendulum swings too far, you have to wonder, what are we fighting for anymore, really?"—Dan Fagin, a *Newsday* reporter

---

Reporters who write about environmental safety believe they're seeing an erosion of access to information about pipelines, chemical plants, and nuclear power.

"This has given the regulated industries a wonderful opportunity. They've never liked right-to-know laws and the Freedom of Information Act, and they're tired of having to release data that have been embarrassing to them," says Dan Fagin, an environmental reporter for *Newsday* and president of the Society of Environmental Journalists.

Fagin, who lost three friends when the World Trade Center towers fell in the terrorist attacks, says the threat of violent terrorism feels very real to him and other New Yorkers. But America, he says, shouldn't give up the right to information gathered by a free press.

"If the pendulum swings too far, you have to wonder, what are we fighting for anymore, really?" he asks.

Civil Liberties Evolve

Controversy surrounded the Bill of Rights from the start. At the 1787 Constitutional Convention, delegates defeated a proposal for a bill of rights. Opponents argued that state constitutions already contained bills of rights and the federal Constitution wouldn't take away those rights.

But voices from the states insisted the new federal government's power needed tempering. Patrick Henry and Thomas Jefferson agreed. Without a Bill of Rights, the states might not have ratified the Constitution and so advocates of a strong federal government agreed to support one. Congress, led by James Madison, eventually wrote the first 10 amendments, which the states ratified in 1791.

As the U.S. Supreme Court interpreted the Bill of Rights and other amendments over the next 200 years, the court's makeup and the politics of the time interplayed to gradually give us what we know today as our civil liberties.

There have been flip-flops: The Fourteenth Amendment, ratified following the Civil War, was not interpreted to extend individual liberty protection to actions from the states until a landmark case in 1925. Before that, the Supreme Court was reluctant to take on state laws.

In 1940, Jehovah's Witnesses were told by the Supreme Court that schools could force their children to salute the flag; then three years later, the court said forced flag salutes were unconstitutional.

In 1961, the Supreme Court told the states that evidence gathered without a legal search warrant could not be admitted at trial, but subsequent cases created exceptions. A woman's right to seek an abortion, protected constitutionally by *Roe v. Wade* in 1973, also has been modified.

"Keeping up with it is stimulating."

The law evolves. How do police, who must enforce the law within changing boundaries, feel about keeping up?

Undercover drug Detective Dan Ervin of the Spokane Police Department thinks about that question as he sits in his unmarked car, eyes glued to a black Mustang that police have a warrant to search.

"The law is a living, breathing organism that changes," Ervin says as he waits with an outfielder's focus. "It has to because society is changing. Keeping up with it is stimulating. It's not frustrating." No barriers have come down from the courts that he can't live with, Ervin says. He tries not to let his own politics affect how he does his job.

"I know I'm more conservative than a lot of people. But who do I serve out here? I serve the community, whether you're a Democrat or a Republican."

An hour later, Ervin and his colleagues find a small rock of crack cocaine in the black Mustang and $2,302 on its driver.

The Mustang driver, seen delivering drugs the previous week, according to the search warrant, goes to jail, where he admits he's hidden something between his buttock cheeks. A baggie of whitish-yellow substance, covered in fecal matter, ends up on a detective's desk. The other drug cops laugh when they hear this over the radio, but they aren't surprised. Hiding contraband this way is something they've seen before. In fact, Washington law specifies that they would need a signed warrant to search a suspect's body cavity. And the search would have to be done by a medical professional.

All this is probably not what James Madison envisioned when he proposed the Fourth Amendment and the rest of the Bill of Rights. The Founders were thinking more about how British customs inspectors had ransacked homes looking for evidence of violations of the Stamp Act.

Thomas Jefferson knew nothing about crack cocaine. Or satellite imagery. Or computer data-mining. He wrote: "A bill of rights is what the people are entitled to against every government on earth."

The American system of government has proved robust enough to handle society's changing problems while protecting individual rights against unchecked government power.

So far, so good.

Can We Be Secure and Free?

BY THOMAS F. POWERS
THE PUBLIC INTEREST, SPRING 2003

> *They that can give up essential liberty to obtain a little temporary safety deserve neither liberty or safety.*—Benjamin Franklin

> *Political liberty consists in security or, at least, in the opinion one has of one's security.*—Montesquieu

Has the war on terror breathed new life into the forces of authoritarianism in America? That certainly is the suggestion of many in today's debate over civil liberties. But the current contours of the debate, in which defenders of liberty oppose those arguing in the name of security, are fundamentally misleading. As it now stands, the controversy is deeply confused and exaggerates the disagreement between parties of good will on both sides. The debate has also set in motion an unnecessary spiral of mistrust that may now be beyond our power to escape. But it may still be possible to clean up some of the confusion that prevails on all sides and sort out what is really at issue.

The first, and thus far the most significant, domestic opposition to government policy in the war on terror has come from civil libertarians. The American Civil Liberties Union and other civil liberties interest groups have mounted widely publicized legal challenges to a number of measures enacted in the wake of the attacks of September 11. The National Lawyer's Guild and the Lawyers Committee for Human Rights, representing lawyers from across the nation, have launched protest efforts. Three hundred law professors signed a widely noticed petition opposing the administration's proposed use of military tribunals. More than 40 cities, towns, and counties (including Denver, Detroit, and San Francisco) have passed resolutions calling for resistance to, and the repeal of, the USA PATRIOT Act (declaring their environs "civil liberties safe zones"). Especially because we live in the wake of a period of ambitious expansions of freedom of speech, civil rights, and due process protections, any claim that our civil liberties are being curtailed or violated cannot but be troubling to this generation of Americans.

But the arguments in response to the concerns of civil libertarians are also powerful. The government's duty in a time of uncertainty and extreme danger, such as the United States now faces, must be to conduct a thorough investigation of the harms done and to minimize potential future threats. After September 11, it is impossible to deny the very real possibility that a terrorist could detonate a nuclear bomb in an American city. Under such circumstances, anything but the most vigorous security policy (foreign and domestic) would be inexcusable.

In the eyes of civil libertarians, the attitude of the government seems to reflect an exclusive concern with security, straining the limits of liberty and leaving it to the courts (and civil libertarian activists) to push the administration back across the line. While professing concern for civil liberties, the Bush administration has not mounted any significant public relations effort to dispel such worries, preferring instead to underscore the necessities of security. By way of contrast, the administration's efforts to reassure Arab and Muslim Americans that their civil rights are secure has been much more vigorous and visible.

We seem . . . to have settled into a debate between the advocates of liberty on the one hand and the defenders of security on the other.

Anatomy of the Debate

We seem then to have settled into a debate between the advocates of liberty on the one hand and the defenders of security on the other. But to begin by assuming a fundamental conflict between liberty and security is to misunderstand the essential logic of liberal politics. In a liberal republic, liberty presupposes security; the point of security is liberty. Liberty and security are, as Assistant Attorney General Viet D. Dinh has put it, "mutually reinforcing goods." Dividing these concerns is not only misleading but has the effect of poisoning public deliberation. In its most extreme form, the debate appears to pit the defenders of liberalism against hostile authoritarian elements that would overthrow it. But this is a very unhelpful exaggeration. The party of security in the current debate is not composed of "authoritarians" who see the war as an opportunity to unchain their pathological illiberal demons. We are all liberals here.

Yet all of us—whether we take the side of security or liberty—are perhaps confused liberals. To see where we stand and what is at stake, we need to disentangle the many strands of argument and layers of history that contribute to our current situation. Since the government policies at issue are as varied and complex as the civil liberties objections to them, I will begin by enumerating the areas of dispute and the actions taken by the administration, Congress, and the courts. I will then bring into focus what is novel and distinctive about this debate, namely that the current war effort (which necessarily emphasizes policing as much as military force) has run headlong into a heightened commitment in American politics to procedural protections of the individual in the courtroom and in dealings with the police. This due process "revolution," I will argue, has produced a new understanding of individual liberty, one which has greatly influenced today's debate. But, perhaps just as important, our public debate is also energized and directed to an important degree by partisan political considerations, and has become polarized along more or less predictable (if, as I will argue, ultimately arbitrary) party lines, tapping into a legacy of the politicization of civil liberties dating back to the Cold War, Vietnam, and the turmoil of the 1960s.

That this heightened rhetoric, raised to the level of constitutional principle, has taken hold in a time of war is unfortunate. But because the opposition between liberty and security rests in fact upon an unwarranted dichotomy, we may be able to find more common ground than the current debate would lead us to believe exists.

Homeland Security Measures

Every war brings with it, according to its particular circumstances, its own distinctive set of civil liberties challenges. The present conflict has posed five main areas of controversy: due process issues, extraordinary detention, the civil rights of noncitizens, government secrecy, and the treatment of terrorist captives outside the United States.

Every war brings with it, according to its particular circumstances, its own distinctive set of civil liberties challenges.

The first and greatest source of concern among civil libertarians arises from the expansion of police powers that make it easier for government agencies to conduct surveillance, use wiretaps and searches, obtain access to personal records, and track and question designated groups. As a result, the current civil liberties debate is distinctive for its novel focus on issues related to due process.

Expanded scope for surveillance is an especially important feature of the new effort. The USA PATRIOT Act (the acronym abbreviates "Uniting and Strengthening America by Providing Appropriate Tools Required to Intercept and Obstruct Terrorism") gives police agencies new authority to conduct expanded telephone and Internet surveillance and loosens 1970s restrictions on the ability of the C.I.A. to engage in domestic surveillance. Under new Department of Justice guidelines that employ a broad definition of terrorism, the F.B.I. may now monitor religious and political groups without specific evidence of wrongdoing (i.e., without "probable cause") in the name of national security. "Operations TIPS" (Terrorist Information and Prevention System), which was debated and ultimately halted in Congress (in an effort notably led by then House Majority Leader Dick Armey), would have encouraged *civilian* surveillance of private persons (its detractors claim it was designed to circumvent the due process restraints ordinarily imposed on the police). Another effort stopped by Congress (at least for the moment) is the Pentagon's "Total Information Awareness" data-mining program, which would examine a variety of public and private databases to search for evidence of terrorist group activity. This effort would follow provisions of the USA PATRIOT Act that make it easier for law enforcement agencies to gain access to various kinds of personal records in the hands of third parties such as schools, libraries, bookstores, doctors, and employers.

The power of the police to track, monitor, and question individuals has also increased. Plans to fingerprint and track electronically Arab and Muslim noncitizens have been announced by the Department of Justice. The new Department of Homeland Security has plans to standardize state drivers' licenses in a move that will, according to critics, effectively create a new "national identity card." The police have also been authorized to question thousands of Arab and Muslim men, without "individualized suspicion" of wrongdoing.

Likewise, search warrants and wiretaps requested in the name of national security may now be granted with a lower standard of proof (without showing of "probable cause"). New rules expand the geographical coverage of search warrants granted on national security grounds, effectively making them national warrants, not limited to the jurisdiction of the court where they are issued. Related rules make wiretap orders more flexible, allowing multiple telephones and cellular phones to be covered under a single judicial authorization. Authorization of "sneak and peek" searches for national security (in which the suspect is unaware that a search has been conducted) requires a lower burden of proof than do searches undertaken in the course of an ordinary criminal investigation.

Added to these expanded police powers are three controversial measures to unify and coordinate the operations of various branches of the government. Most notably, the USA PATRIOT Act authorizes the F.B.I. and C.I.A. to cooperate and share information much more closely, bringing together the work of intelligence and law enforcement agencies that had been intentionally separated a generation ago in order to protect civil liberties. To integrate the domestic policing effort in the war on terror, the Department of Homeland Security is expected to provide local law enforcement with much more information gathered from national law enforcement agencies. Finally, the Department of Homeland Security is also assessing the extent to which military forces may be used to aid civilian law enforcement efforts, in the face of the 1878 Posse Comitatus Act prohibiting domestic use of the military.

Civil libertarians are concerned that this expansion of government power endangers the rights of individuals before the judicial system and diminishes the "expectation of privacy" of those under investigation. Another area of concern is the government's treatment of those individuals (almost exclusively noncitizens) who have been detained for extended periods of time as part of the investigation into the attacks of September 11 and other terrorist activities.

While the Department of Justice insists that all detainees have been accorded the procedural protections due to them, civil libertarians claim that at least some of the detainees have been held without knowledge of the charges against them, without access to the courts, and without access to legal counsel (or, if given access to lawyers, without attorney-client privacy). Moreover, detainees have been held under extraordinary legal justifications: Those not held for minor immigration violations were charged with often trivial criminal offenses or were held on "material witness" warrants used only rarely for mafia trials.

While most of these procedural questions have been raised in relation to noncitizens, two prominent cases involve Americans. Yaser Hamdi, a U.S. citizen who was captured after fighting with the Taliban in Afghanistan, and José Padilla, arrested in Chicago for his alleged involvement in a plot to detonate a "dirty bomb," have been designated "enemy combatants" by the administration. This designation permits Hamdi and Padilla to be held without

---

While people may be willing to contemplate a trade-off between liberty and security, a curtailment of civil rights may prove more troubling.

---

criminal charges, under indefinite detention, and without access to the courts. Civil libertarians claim that this detention violates the Constitution's *habeas corpus* guarantee (which can be suspended only by an act of Congress).

The suspension of ordinary legal procedure for mainly noncitizens (but some citizens as well) has led civil libertarians to raise a broader set of questions concerning the rights of noncitizens. They are troubled that many of the expanded powers of the police single out specific groups—male Arab and Muslim noncitizens—for special treatment. While people may be willing to contemplate a trade-off between liberty and security, a curtailment of civil rights may prove more troubling. The new security policies have also been accompanied by an intensification of internal government secrecy. The surveillance, wiretapping, and investigation of private records that go with the new national security effort are necessarily to be done in secret. These policy innovations are perceived by critics to be in line with a general spirit of secretiveness said to pervade the executive branch. The Immigration and Naturalization Service (INS) has attempted to keep secret any deportation hearings related to the war on terror. The Attorney General has encouraged all executive agencies to resist Freedom of Information Act requests where possible. Perhaps most visibly, the Department of Justice has itself consistently refused to provide information about those being detained as part of its ongoing investigations.

Last but not least, civil libertarians voice concerns about the treatment of suspected terrorists captured abroad in military engagements or arrested by foreign allies. As many as several thousand captives have been held by the American government or in its name since the attacks of September 11. Though the government insists that those detained are being treated humanely, they have been denied the status of prisoners of war (labeled instead "enemy combatants") and the protections of the Geneva Convention that go with the P.O.W. designation. The treatment of some 600 captives at a military base in Guantanamo Bay briefly gained media attention. More troubling for civil libertarians are reports of the use of methods that may amount to torture to extract information from captives held in remote locations (whether by officials of the American military or intelligence services or by agents of governments with dubious human rights records). While Harvard law professor Alan Dershowitz is willing to contemplate justified nonlethal torture, most other civil libertarians are not. Finally, the special status of terrorist captives has made likely the resurrection of military tribunals to try them. This has been vigorously opposed on the grounds that such tribunals smack in some general sense of authoritarianism. But more specifically, civil libertarians protest that military tribunals have lower standards of procedural protections for the accused and have a greater tendency to secrecy.

> *The debate has . . . been shaped by the unusual character of this war and the unique task facing the government.*

A Reasonable Response

The many challenges raised by the war on terror make the debate about it multifaceted and complex. This complexity itself is perhaps one reason a simple "liberty versus security" framework has gained traction. Instead of grappling with the many difficult issues involved, each side can simply appeal to a single criterion of concern. Advocates of security see in recent government policies admirable vigor; civil libertarians see them simply as a long train of abuses.

Yet the debate has also been shaped by the unusual character of this war and the unique task facing the government. Because the enemy is a terrorist organization operating in part on American soil, the response is unavoidably at least as much a matter for law enforcement as for the military. Because the terrorists have proven themselves capable of striking in the face of less vigorous and less coordinated policing efforts, some greater, more tightly orchestrated effort is manifestly required. That the government's investigation targets Arabs and Muslims cannot but make Americans uncomfortable. Yet this emphasis reflects certain undeniable facts concerning the identity of the participants in the attacks of September 11 (and not racist or ethnic or religious prejudice, which the administration has indeed made a concerted effort to declaim). Since information can be misused with great potential costs, the government has not surprisingly adopted a policy of heightened secrecy. Likewise, military tribunals fulfill specific needs imposed by the current conflict, for which civilian courts were not designed.

This is not to suggest that every element of the government's effort is therefore sound. One can reasonably ask questions about every detail of these measures. But the general shape of the government's response is a logical result of September 11, and would have followed regardless of who led the effort. Whatever one thinks about the new set of challenges to civil liberties in America, these challenges are not the result of some paranoid "authoritarian" agenda, pursued by government officials for its own sake.

Congress and the Courts Weigh In

Evidence for the reasonableness of the new policies is to be found in the support garnered for them in Congress and the courts. On the whole, members of Congress have taken an aggressive stance in authorizing new government powers to fight the war on terror. It is true that Senate Judiciary Committee hearings on military tribunals and detentions held in November and December of 2001 prompted some revisions to the rules governing military tribunals. Similarly, Operation TIPS and (for now) the Pentagon's Total Information Awareness program have been blocked by Congress. But more striking is the overwhelming support Congress gave to both the USA PATRIOT Act (which passed in the Senate 98 to 1 and in the House 337 to 79) and the creation of the Department of Homeland Security (passing in the Senate 90 to 9 and in the House 299 to 121). The wide-ranging debate in Congress over extraordinary detentions and military tribunals has proven the exception rather than the rule. This may change if civil liberties issues become increasingly politicized, but for now the reaction from within Congress has been tame compared to the claims of civil libertarian activists.

Similarly, in the judiciary, several lower court decisions striking down government policies in the name of protecting civil liberties gained wide publicity, but almost all of these have been overturned on appeal. The Foreign Intelligence Surveillance Court issued a rare ruling that seemed to call into question several important provisions of the USA PATRIOT Act, only to be reversed by a ruling of the secret Foreign Intelligence Surveillance Court of Review. A demand for information on detainees held in New Jersey was upheld at the trial level but struck down by the state court of appeals. The power of the government to freeze accounts and seize records of groups suspected of having ties to terrorists was upheld in federal court. A challenge to the government's authority to detain "enemy combatants" without prisoner-of-war status at Guantanamo Bay was dismissed. Overturning a lower court ruling, the U.S. Court of Appeals for the Fourth Circuit upheld the government's indefinite detention of U.S. citizen and designated "enemy combatant" Yaser Hamdi. In the José Padilla case, in something of a compromise, a federal judge in Manhattan ruled that the government may hold a U.S. citizen indefinitely without charge as an "enemy combatant" but that the detainee has a right to an attorney. The U.S. Courts of Appeal for the Third and Sixth Circuits have issued contradictory opinions over whether immigration deportation hearings may be closed to the public (the Supreme Court may eventually decide the issue). The only complete victory for civil libertarians in the courts thus far is a federal court ruling ordering the government to release the names of those detained as part of the investigation of the events of September 11, a ruling that is currently under appeal.

This survey of the distinctive responses, the stances taken by various branches of government, and the areas of conflict is a necessary beginning point. But a fuller understanding of what is at issue behind the current debate requires a broader historical and theoretical analysis.

The Due Process Revolution

To comprehend the intensity of the current civil libertarian critique, we must consider recent constitutional history. Testifying before the Senate Judiciary Committee, Georgetown University law professor Neal Katyal insisted that military tribunals were unconstitutional. The striking basis of his claim was the *irrelevance* of the long line of Supreme Court precedents pronouncing their constitutional validity. In Katyal's view, we could disregard these cases because they had been "decided before the due process revolution in the federal courts, which took place only in the 1960s." Though not the only questions raised by the war on terror, due process issues comprise the bulk of the controversy to date and are likely to continue to occupy a central position in the future. This is the first major and prolonged military conflict the United States has faced since Vietnam, and it offers a unique test of our commitment to recent innovations in due process protections.

The heart of the due process revolution of the 1960s was the extension of the protections afforded to criminal suspects in the Fourth through Eighth Amendments to the Constitution, previously applied only at the national level, down to the level of state and local laws, courts, and police practices. This was accomplished by means of the due process clause of the Fourteenth Amendment, and proceeded in a piecemeal fashion by the "incorporation" of the Bill of Rights. Although this process had begun earlier, in the view of conservatives, the Warren Court in the 1960s essentially legislated into existence a uniform national standard superceding (or at least supplementing) the sometimes less ambitious protections of the criminally accused already in place at the state and local level. Several elements of the newly created constitutional standards were especially controversial. Various law enforcement practices relating to surveillance, wiretapping, searches, interrogation, and self-incrimination were declared unconstitutional. The widespread and more aggressive use of the "exclusionary rule" (excluding constitution-ally "tainted" evidence or testimony, instead of penalizing in some other way police officers who break the rules) magnified further the impact of the new reforms. Other famous Warren Court decisions championed the nationalization of the rights of defendants to reasonable bail and to legal counsel. In 1972, the Court seemed to go so far as to declare the death penalty unconstitutional.

Though many of the more controversial Warren Court holdings have been significantly narrowed in subsequent years, it is certainly the case that due process rights are a much more important part of our national political debate than they were prior to the 1960s. A new set of constitutional issues has emerged for civil libertarians to champion. As one constitutional law textbook proclaims: "Due process of law ranks with freedom and equality in the American trinity of civil liberties." Indeed, one may speak of a distinct new form of "due process civil libertarianism," the achievement of which has been the elevation of a set of legal procedures to a new, heightened level of moral concern and protection.

> *Limitations applied to due process rights today are not viewed, even by most civil libertarians, as a way to stifle voices of opposition to the war effort.*

We can see the special character of our current situation, with its novel emphasis on due process, by comparing it to earlier civil liberties crises in our history. The attempt by the administration of John Adams to use the Alien and Sedition Acts to quell public disagreement with its policy toward the French Revolution centered on the very idea of a "loyal opposition." The eventual defeat of Adams's Federalist party in the election of 1800 and its ultimate collapse as a viable force on the national stage seemed to settle the issue decisively on the side of open and free debate of wartime questions. Lincoln's extraconstitutional measures during the Civil War—commencing hostilities and suspending the writ of *habeas corpus* without explicit Congressional authorization—raised a variety of issues, including what we would today term due process considerations. But, during the Civil War, due process violations were viewed as less important than violations of free speech, freedom of the press, and the elementary rights of political opposition. During World War I, passage of Espionage and Sedition Acts once again put free speech front and center. World War I saw the Supreme Court's first free speech rulings as well as the formation of the American Civil Liberties Union. During World War II, the policies of the Roosevelt administration raised relatively few civil liberties questions. However, the internment of Japanese Americans (upheld by the Supreme Court in a decision that still stands, however notoriously) has been widely judged in retrospect to have been a colossal civil rights failure.

It seems fair to say that America has learned several important lessons from its previous wars. The issues we face today do not arise because wartime fears and patriotic zeal have spawned repression of political opposition or freedom of speech, as with the Alien and Sedition Acts of 1798, the Civil War, and World War I. Limitations applied to due process rights today are not viewed, even by most civil libertarians, as a way to stifle voices of opposition to the war effort. While troubling civil rights issues have surfaced, the differences between the actions of the Bush administration and the mass internment of Japanese Americans during World War II are as important as they are obvious. The distinctive focus of the current controversy is on questions of due process. And it is in regard to these policies that we will likely be judged in the future.

What is a due process civil libertarian?

The centrality of due process in today's debate is thus novel, reflecting the specific character of the current conflict as well as recent constitutional developments. It is also somewhat strange. What is a "due process civil libertarian"? And how are we to understand this new form of liberal idealism that has been so starkly revealed by the pressures of war?

While it is easy to see the lofty appeal of freedom of worship, freedom of speech, and civil rights, the protections of due process are less inspiring. It is true that due process protections are connected in obvious ways to the general ideal of limited government enshrined in the Constitution. But are there not important distinctions to be drawn between those constitutional features that are more and less fundamental to this ideal? Wrongful convictions and police abuse are obvious evils, and their attempted avoidance a great benefit of a humane, civilized society. But can resistance to such (ultimately unavoidable) failings of a legal order really generate the same sort of moral idealism as the other central features of our constitutional order? Crime too is an evil, but we have no corresponding name or high moral praise for the avoidance of it. Moreover, unlike freedom of religion, freedom of speech, and civil rights, issues relating to due process do not involve the distinctive *substance* of policy or the content of political life in a liberal republic. These are issues that arise in the administration of justice in any and every political order.

Of course, resisting abuses by the courts, police, and other agents of the state *has* attained a place of high moral stature in American life. But this is evidence of a strange and tantalizing aspect of liberal democratic life of the past century: an idealization of even the most mundane of liberal democratic principles. The Enlightenment philosophers who first formulated the principles of liberalism were a realistic lot who hoped to erect a successful new order by appealing to the universal desire for security, prosperity, comfort, and some minimal level of recognition of the dignity of ordinary citizens. But our ever more zealous moralizing of even due process, one of the more mundane principles of the social contract (the social contract itself reflecting a relatively unexalted view of political life), seems to suggest that the originators of liberalism underestimated mankind's deep longings for moral elevation. The moralization of due process has followed the elevation of freedom of speech over the past century. Free speech itself was originally justified mainly in terms of its contribution to political opposition; today, it is typically tied to loftier notions of freedom of the mind or artistic creation.

However the idealization of due process protections took place, their newly exalted status helps to explain the origins of the current debate. But so too does something much more broadly shared by Americans that now complements due process civil libertarianism, namely, the ideal of limited government at the heart of the Constitution. No people that takes limited government to heart so thoroughly can be unaffected by the awesome exertion of state power in time of war. The very idea that government is subordinate to citizens may seem at risk. This reaction may be partly a sign of democratic resentment against the state, but it is also more than that. It is perhaps a measure of the vigor of the basic moral instincts of liberalism.

> *The moralization of due process has followed the elevation of freedom of speech over the past century.*

The Politicization of Civil Liberties

But there is also another explanation for the shape of today's debate over civil liberties. This debate taps into much broader and deeper partisan disagreements that have little to do with the merits of the claims made on either side, and that go back 40 or 50 years to a very different set of foreign policy and international security questions. While it is important to resist the cynical view now dominant among constitutional scholars which reduces every legal controversy to raw "politics," any discussion that ignores the politicization of civil liberties in America leaves out an essential part of the picture.

The extent to which the debate over civil liberties and the war corresponds to partisan divisions is best explained by the political history of the past half century, not by any deep ideological differences between the two parties. A new constellation of issues took hold of partisan politics in the 1960s and 1970s, through the trauma of a decade of civil rights protest, the humiliation of military defeat in Vietnam, and the forced resignation of a Republican president. Institutional reforms authored by Democrats, which Republicans could not but accept under the circumstances, locked in a series of opposed partisan positions that were essentially arbitrary, dependent more on the immediate circumstances than on any deep differences of principle.

If the 1960s was a decade of bitter political turmoil, the 1970s saw debates over constitutional and institutional issues that elevated the battles of the previous decade to a new level. During the Nixon administration, and perhaps more intensely after Nixon's humiliation, the office of the presidency itself came to bear an important portion of the blame for policy outcomes, both foreign and domestic, in an era when each party held a different branch of government. Democrats who had hailed Franklin D. Roosevelt as an enlightened statesman a generation earlier now decried the "imperial" presidency and called for a vigorous reassertion of Congressional authority. Democrats sought, and Republicans deplored, constitutional and institutional reforms that still influence the positions of the two parties today. Restriction of the president's war-making power was enshrined in the new framework of the War Powers Resolution, which passed over Nixon's veto. The year before, Democrats sponsored the Case Act, which limited the president's perceived overuse of executive agreements (and circumvention of the Senate's treaty-approval power). Similar motives and partisan alignments impelled reform of the C.I.A. and the establishment of new intelligence oversight powers for the House and Senate. The Democrats' desire to tame the presidency in the domestic arena (and Republicans' opposition to the same) is most vividly exemplified in the debate over the Budget and Impoundment Act of 1974, which asserted a greater role for Congress in the budget process and restricted the presidential impoundment power used so vigorously by Nixon. Partisan divisions also matched constitutional alignments in debates over issues of executive privilege (*U.S. v. Nixon*) and governmental secrecy (the Freedom of Information Act).

Due process issues—questions of the legitimacy of the authority of the state in general and of the police in particular—are bound up in this broader political dynamic governing constitutional issues. Due process issues have also been tied to, and have stood in for, other more deeply rooted political differences concerning wealth and economic justice. The connection can be seen directly in the case of the provision of legal counsel for the indigent, but also more broadly in the struggle over the Great Society agenda (where issues of crime and criminality were often connected to issues of poverty and other socio-economic inequalities). In this way the debate over rights of the criminally accused became, at least in part, a proxy for partisan disagreements over a variety of social policy issues.

Disputes over civil liberties questions that have arisen in the years since reenact the powerful and dramatic morality play of the 1960s and 1970s. Divisions rooted in efforts by each side to blame the other for perceived harms, indignities, and injustices left a wound in America that still has not healed. It is in this context that Republicans have come to see themselves as defenders of governmental authority in security and military matters while Democrats see themselves as the party fundamentally suspicious of institutional "authoritarianism."

Recent evidence of the power of partisanship to shape civil liberties debates is provided by the brief but fierce public controversy over military tribunals in the fall of 2001. In the face of the sudden collapse of Taliban resistance in Afghanistan, and the immediate necessity of dealing with the likely capture of Al Qaeda leaders, President Bush issued an executive order authorizing the use of military tribunals.

> *Due process questions in particular do not inevitably divide along partisan lines.*

Necessarily acting in haste, the administration modeled its executive order on the one issued by President Roosevelt in 1942. As the testimony of legal experts on both the left and right ultimately revealed, from a constitutional point of view there was nothing particularly controversial about the use of military tribunals. A long line of judicial precedents upheld their use, and even Harvard law professor Laurence Tribe, who spoke out loudly against Bush's order, conceded its essential legality.

But the outcry over the order was nothing less than clamorous, a development that took the Bush administration by surprise. The issue seems to have provided Democrats (if not only Democrats) with an opportunity to criticize *some* aspect of a Republican president's conduct of a war that had proven, to that point, to be essentially beyond criticism. This is not to say that Democrats' arguments from principle were disingenuous or *reducible* to partisan concerns, but it is to insist that the political dimension be seen for what it is—an accident of history.

It makes no more sense to say that the war on terror proves that Republicans are in principle less concerned than Democrats about due process (or, for example, about the respective institutional prerogatives of the president and Congress) than it does to insist that the policies of World War I prove that Democrats were less committed to freedom of speech than were Republicans, or that World War II shows that the Roosevelt administration was less committed to civil rights. At moments of crisis, parties can fall into defending (or criticizing) certain constitutional propositions, and the divisions that emerge at such moments may be enduring. That the current debate between liberty and security is to some important degree the result of misdirected partisanship is a good reason to question the emerging divide.

Generally speaking, there is nothing in the basic principles of either the Republican or Democratic parties that requires the partisan alignment on these issues that seems to be taking hold. Due process questions in particular do not inevitably divide along partisan lines. Matters pertaining to the proper enforcement of the law, as laid out in the Fourth through the Eighth Amendments, have no necessary connection to substantive differences between the parties over the content of the law. Similarly, the parties would appear to have no intrinsic relation to either security or liberty. Indeed, one might easily imagine the divide falling the other way: Should not Republicans, skeptical of government, also be skeptical of the enforcement arm of the state? Should not Democrats' faith in government also extend to those enforcing the policies of the state?

That the partisan divide on these questions is ultimately incoherent also helps to explain why it is so commonly crossed-over by Democrats as well as Republicans. As I have noted, both the USA PATRIOT Act and the Homeland Security Act had overwhelming bipartisan support. That Republican Dick Armey was instrumental in stopping Operation TIPS in Congress illustrates the potential for partisan flexibility on these issues. Indeed, during the Clinton years, it was conservative groups who in the name of civil liberties criticized efforts by the federal government to create a national identification card and database enabling law enforcement to investigate and track individuals suspected of terrorist activity. During the early scuffle over military tribunals and related issues, it was conservative columnist William Safire who first cried "tyranny." Students of the Supreme Court are well aware that the standard division of justices into conservative, moderate, and liberal breaks down on due process issues. Judges who are predictably liberal on other issues are often surprisingly untroubled by vigorous policing, and conservatives are at times more solicitous of the rights of the accused than are their more liberal counterparts.

But although many people in public life do not fall into a simple or absolute partisan position on these issues, just such a divide threatens to become the common sense of our public debate, especially for the ideologues of either party. Whether a partisan political division in constitutional debates is useful or not depends on whether there is in fact anything of substance at stake. Even where division on constitutional questions ultimately stands in for other, more deeply rooted political divisions, an airing of arguments from principle may serve beneficial purposes: The community may return to its founding principles; dangerous political energies may be channeled into less explosive issues. But where there is nothing fundamental at stake, politicized constitutional issues can create disagreement, hostility, and mistrust. We seem now to be witnessing the ossifying of another layer of American constitutional debate in which the Republican party plays the sober, "realist" party of security in wartime while Democrats (or a significant segment of the party) take for themselves the stance of protecting "principles" and liberty.

Liberty and Security

For Americans, a debate over questions of liberty and security in wartime is necessarily a constitutional debate. Yet the Constitution was shaped by liberal political theory, which tells us that liberty and security are, if not equivocal terms, surely no more than two closely related aspects of the same basic understanding of the purposes of political life. Liberal theory begins with the assertion that individuals have rights, and that individuals surrender the complete liberty that is theirs by nature only on the promise that social life will be organized around the protection of their rights. Liberalism requires the state to protect citizens against a variety of dangers. First, the state must protect individuals from one another through the mechanisms of criminal law and the protections of national defense. But it must also protect citizens from those who possess authority in an organized society, i.e., the government. In Madison's famous and more succinct formulation in *Federalist* 51: "In framing a government which is to be administered by men over men, the great difficulty lies in this: you must first enable the government to control the governed; and in the next place oblige it to control itself." From this point of view, it is clear that there is not so much a "tension" between liberty and security as there is a duality of our concern with security, on the one hand, and with liberty, on the other.

This duality is captured by John Locke and Montesquieu, two architects of early liberal thought and, indirectly through their influence on the Founders, of the U.S. Constitution. Spelling out the classic formulation of the social contract, Locke emphasizes precisely the relationship between liberty and security, suggesting, indeed, the necessity of the latter for the enjoyment of the former.

> If man in the State of Nature be so free, as has been said; if he be absolute Lord of his own Person and Possessions, equal to the greatest, and subject to no Body, why will he part with his Freedom? . . . To which 'tis obvious to Answer, that though in the state of Nature he hath such a right, yet the Enjoyment of it is very uncertain, and constantly exposed to the Invasion of others. . . . This makes him willing to quit a Condition, which however free, is full of fears and continual dangers: And 'tis not without reason, that he seeks out, and is willing to joyn in Society with others who are already united, or have a mind to unite for the mutual *Preservation* of their Lives, Liberties, and Estates.

Discussing the people's right of revolution, Locke goes so far as to identify "provid[ing] for their own Safety and Security" as being "the end for which they are in society." Locke does not of course advocate security at any cost—tyrannical government is for him worse than the insecurity of the state of nature. But Locke points out what we seem to have forgotten: At the very least, security is the essential precondition of liberty.

Similarly, in his treatment of the subject in *The Spirit of the Laws*, Montesquieu goes so far as to define political liberty in terms of security.

> Political liberty consists in security or, at least, in the opinion one has of one's security. This security is never more attacked than by public or private accusations. Therefore, the citizen's

liberty depends principally on the goodness of the criminal laws . . . The knowledge [of criminal law] . . . is of more concern to mankind than anything else in the world.

Today, in contrast, the relationship of liberty and security is denied by civil libertarians, and the terms have been torn asunder by all participants in the debate. "Security" has come to refer one-sidedly to the threat from criminals, and in the debate over the war on terror it has come to refer to the threat from external enemies. "Liberty," in contrast, is held to refer to protection from the abuses of the police and other agents of the state. This is an exaggerated, arbitrary, and unhelpful separation of these key terms. Every threat, from whatever source, is as much a threat to our liberty as it is to our security.

The crucial point is that liberty and security are rooted in the same elemental concerns of the liberal democratic understanding of the origins and essential justification of organized social life. American democracy would be done a service if we would use exclusively either the language of security or the language of liberty. A debate, for example, over how to weigh the threat military tribunals pose to the liberties of war-crimes suspects against the threat terrorists pose to the liberties of citizens would be more clear-sighted than is our current division of these issues along liberty versus security lines. Similarly, sorting out the impact of new police powers under the USA PATRIOT Act in terms of security against terrorism on the one hand, and security against errors of state prosecution or police abuses on the other, would more accurately capture what is at stake. What we need is to reframe our discussion around the decidedly unglamorous task of balancing one threat to liberty against other threats to liberty, one threat to security against other threats to security. I do not wish to suggest that recasting the question in these terms will easily settle the many difficult choices that must be made in the war on terror, but it would permit us to face them more clearly and without fearing that we are being either unprincipled or soft-headed.

Beyond Partisanship?

The present danger is not that one side or the other will unjustly benefit from the relative rhetorical strength of either liberty or security. Indeed, both sides are content to continue to argue as they do since appeals to liberty and security are more or less evenly matched (necessarily so, one might say, given their shared origin). The problem is the reopening of old wounds of mistrust in America, the healing of which could instead be an important benefit of the common effort we are making in the war on terror. The worst aspects of a raw and empty partisanship are given opportunities precisely where they should be denied.

The intense reaction of civil libertarians to the demands of the war on terror is to some degree a sign of genuine progress in America in taking those aspects of limited government pertaining to the police and other agents of the state more seriously. It also reflects, more generally, a natural reaction on the part of all citizens to the awesome exercise of state power in time of war. So far so good. But instead of ensuring that all sides of these complicated questions are heard, the current debate has exaggerated disagreement and launched a dialectic of mutual recrimination and mistrust, now elevated to the level of "constitutional" conflict. What ought to be a practical question of balancing freedom from terrorism with freedom from unnecessary state power becomes instead a pointless game of blame-casting that reawakens the old partisan divisions of the Vietnam era.

> *Civil libertarians must drop the idea that they alone argue from high principle.*

The debate needs to be demoralized. Civil libertarians must drop the idea that they alone argue from high principle. Seeing more clearly the dependence of liberty on security would undercut the tendency to see every increase in police powers as inherently suspect. If they had a proper understanding of the relation between liberty and security, civil libertarians would not depict their opponents as enemies of liberty or as advocates of unbridled "authoritarianism," a view divorced from reality. The very commitment of civil libertarians to liberty should in fact make them defenders of security—to protecting citizens as much from harms inflicted by criminals and external enemies as from abuses by the state.

Conservatives who argue mainly on grounds of security should see the deep moral limitations of their stance. To argue for security "against" liberty in a liberal democracy can never be more than a temporary, defensive position. Security is a weighty premise to stand upon, but should not be seen to stand in opposition to liberty. In other words, defenders of the government's policies should avoid deferring to the outline of the issues favored by civil libertarians. Conservatives do after all take seriously the concerns of liberty, and the Republican party aspires to be the party of limited government. Conservatives ought to assert their own civil libertarian credentials, confident that their commitment to security entails a commitment to liberty as well.

Such advice, though warranted, is perhaps unlikely to be heeded. It may depend too heavily on a level of good will that our country cannot at this point muster. The confusion and recrimination arising from the false conflict between liberty and security over due process issues may well hold sway. In that case, we may have to resign ourselves to nothing more than seeing the debate for what it is.

Better Safe Than Sorry

By Amitai Etzioni
The Weekly Standard, July 21, 2003

The Bush Administration is incessantly criticized, and not only from the left, for a variety of safety measures it introduced in the wake of the 2001 terrorist attacks. Senator Patrick Leahy, for example, said in November 2001, "We don't protect ourselves by bending or even shredding our Constitution." And a *New York Times* editorial the same month claimed that the president "is eroding the very values and principles he seeks to protect, including the rule of law." Almost daily, someone bemoans the "death of privacy" or the rise of the "surveillance society."

The administration has chosen not to respond to most of these allegations, and when it has responded, it has tended to be tone deaf. And whatever one thinks about mining private data banks to identify suspicious patterns of activity, calling a program designed to do this Total Information Awareness (TIA) only played into the critics' hands.

A careful examination of the new homeland-protection policies finds that they are not all cut from one constitutional, legal, or ethical cloth. Many were overdue when they were finally enacted in the wake of 9/11; several others are also quite reasonable; a few raise troubling questions and at least one useful innovation the administration has yet to adopt.

Before any Cook's tour of the major new measures can begin, a few general points are in order. The key question is often framed as: How far should we be willing to sacrifice our individual rights in order to enhance our safety? But it's a mistake to think of homeland security as a zero sum game, where 100 percent of the turf belongs to rights, and every new safety measure amounts to an intrusion to be justified. To realize how prejudicial this approach is, ask the opposite, equally loaded, question: How far should we be willing to sacrifice our security in order to enhance our rights?

At the heart of the matter is the observation that under the Constitution, no right is absolute. Indeed, protecting the public interest—especially the public safety—is as legitimate as protecting individual rights. Thus, the Fourth Amendment states, "The right of the people to be secure in their persons, houses, papers, and effects, against unreasonable searches and seizures, shall not be violated." That is, the Fourth Amendment recognizes that some searches are reasonable—those deemed to serve a compelling public interest. They do not violate anyone's rights, because the Constitution never gave anyone an absolute right not to be searched.

There is a considerable legal literature about what is "reasonable," with many differences of opinion. By and large, it comes down to an admittedly vague notion: what a reasonable person would consider reasonable. One thing, however, is not in doubt: Much of what was unreasonable before 9/11 ceased to be so that morning.

Measures That Were Overdue

Many of the new safety measures simply bring the law into line with technological developments. These should have been introduced years ago. The most important of these changes involve the Foreign Intelligence Surveillance Act (FISA), enacted in the far-away days of 1978. FISA provides guidelines under which a federal agent can obtain authorization to conduct surveillance for "foreign intelligence purposes." These purposes include protecting Americans from acts of foreign powers, occurring within the United

---

Much of what was unreasonable before 9/11 ceased to be so that morning.

States, or their agents (such as terrorists), whether foreign or American. A major tool of surveillance is the wiretap.

Historically, a wiretap was authorized for a given phone, usually the phone in the suspect's home or office. In recent decades, people have acquired multiple phones, cell phones, and e-mail, but federal officials conducting surveillance under FISA could not follow a suspect as he moved from one instrument to another—not without a separate court order for each communication device. The USA Patriot Act, enacted in October 2001, amended FISA to allow "roving surveillance authority," making it legal for agents to follow the suspect whatever instrument he uses.

Unless you believe that terrorists are entitled to benefit from new technologies but law enforcement must not catch up, this measure is entirely reasonable. Moreover, the critics' claim that surveillance orders are promiscuously granted simply doesn't stand up. Nearly 40 million foreigners visit the United States each year, according to the Commerce Department, yet the FISA court issued little more than 1,000 surveillance orders in 2002—after 9/11— Attorney General Ashcroft reported to the Senate Judiciary Committee in March 2003.

Believe it or not, before 9/11 the regulations that allowed public authorities to record or trace e-mail were interpreted by Department of Justice lawyers as requiring a court order from every jurisdiction through which an e-mail message traveled. This was a holdover from the days when phone lines were local; warrants for phone taps were granted by local authorities and had only a local reach. But today, e-mail messages zoom around by a variety of routes. Now, thanks to the Patriot Act, nationwide tracing and recording orders are permitted under FISA. That is, law enforcement authorities may finally catch up with the technological features of e-mail. Anybody who sees a civil rights violation here should have his vision checked.

Few changes in the laws and regulations after 9/11 have raised more ire than new Department of Justice guidelines permitting the FBI to conduct surveillance of political and religious organizations. The new guidelines, introduced in May 2002, state, "For the purpose of detecting or preventing terrorist activities, the FBI is authorized to visit any place and attend any event that is open to the public, on the same terms and conditions as members of the public generally." Civil libertarians are still fixated on the fact that more than a generation ago the FBI infiltrated some fringe groups (such as the Ku Klux Klan and the Black Panthers) and tapped the phones of civil rights leaders like Martin Luther King Jr. But that was a different FBI, one run by J. Edgar Hoover, accountable to no one, feared by presidents and legislators because of files Hoover kept on their personal lives and because he succeeded in building a public cult around himself. The reforms of the mid-1970s barred FBI agents from so much as attending a public event or entering a public space to observe the goings-on there unless they were investigating a specific crime.

The absurd result was that agents charged with protecting a community were unable to inform themselves firsthand about inflammatory elements in its midst. In particular, terrorists could meet and recruit in places of worship without any fear of being overheard by public authorities. As it turned out, the danger was far from theoretical. A score of people were recruited at mosques in Britain to fight with the Taliban, and some of the 9/11 hijackers were recruited at a mosque in Hamburg, according to German security sources. Since 9/11 several American mosques have been investigated for links to terrorism, including two in the Seattle area and one near St. Louis.

Before 9/11 a Chinese wall separated intelligence agencies, such as the CIA and National Security Agency, from law enforcement, above all the FBI. As Attorney General Ashcroft put it in his July 2002 testimony before the Senate, "A criminal investigator examining a terrorist attack could not coordinate with an intelligence officer investigating the same suspected terrorists." The barriers between agencies, Ashcroft said, prevented cooperation and coordination. Michael Hayden, the director of the NSA, told a recent meeting of the Council on Foreign Relations in Washington that his staff were repeatedly drilled in not sharing "raw information" (which included names and addresses and other identifying marks) with anybody.

Since 9/11 the walls dividing the intelligence collection and law enforcement agencies have been largely removed. A major factor was a 2002 ruling by the FISA court that permitted informa-tion-sharing between intelligence agents and criminal investigators under FISA. And a new culture is being fostered, one that puts a premium on the very collaboration that once was avoided. Turf battles have not disap-

> *It is good to know that now . . . the left hand is allowed to know what the right hand has found out.*

peared, but there is a growing appreciation that the enemy is not the other agency, but bin Laden and his followers. Attorney General Ashcroft is rhapsodic about the new culture, describing it as "capable of adaptation, secured by accountability, nurtured by cooperation, built on coordination, and rooted in our Constitutional liberties." Even without such Hollywood music in the background, it is good to know that now, as a rule, the left hand is allowed to know what the right hand has found out.

Measures That Are Reasonable After 9/11

A few measures that arguably were not needed before 9/11 are now slowly, woefully slowly, being introduced. Prominent among them is a tracking system for foreigners who come to the United States to study. Before 9/11 the United States did not check whether those who came to the country for a defined period of time, say on a student visa, left at the end of the period. Many did not leave, but there was no way of knowing who they were or what they were up to. Actually, a partial tracking system with a mouthful of a name, the Student and Exchange Visitor Information System (SEVIS), was mandated by Congress as far back as 1996, but widespread opposition from colleges and civil libertarians prevented its implementation. No funds were appropriated until the passage of the Patriot Act. The new Internet-based student tracking system requires colleges to verify whether the students they are expecting actually show up. The system is plagued with technical difficulties (when many colleges sign on, the computer system slows to a crawl), procedural delays (to participate, a college must be certified by the INS), and political opposition (several deans of students complain that they are being made to spy for the government). And colleges fear scaring off foreign students, who often pay full fare.

Given that several of the hijackers came to the United States on the pretext that their purpose was to study, and given the large number of students from the terrorists' countries of origin, the tracking system is fully justified. Once debugged, SEVIS should entail minimal bureaucratic burdens; the scrutiny, moreover, falls upon people who are not Americans and who have come here of their own free will, knowing in advance that they would be tracked. Indeed, some kind of tracking system is in place in many democracies. In several E.U. countries, for instance, aliens who relocate are required to register with the local police within 30 days. In the age of international terrorism, some tracking capability is needed so security forces can do their job.

The most important change in law enforcement since 9/11 is that the FBI has shifted its focus from prosecution to prevention. This policy shift comes from the White House. It reorients the agency from collecting information after a crime has been committed to stopping terrorist attacks before they take place. The reason the shift is portentous is that, while prosecution deals with suspects, prevention often entails stirring the pot in the belief that something in it needs to be disturbed. In such cases, a considerable number of people who are not themselves suspected of any wrongdoing may be put through some kind of wringer in order to try to upset a plot that authorities have reason to believe is being hatched.

Thus, in late 2001, on instructions from the Department of Justice, U.S. attorney's offices throughout the nation sent letters to some 5,000 men who had come from countries where Al Qaeda is present or active and who had entered the United States on nonimmigrant (work, tourist, or student) visas, requesting that they present themselves to be interviewed. The purpose of the interviews was to solicit information the government might use in thwarting attacks. Also, it was assumed that there were probably some bad dudes among these men, and that interviews might help ferret them out or scare them into leaving the country. In March 2002, Attorney General Ashcroft reported that the interviews had been productive, saying they "provided us with a number of leads which we think to be very important, and helped us establish relationships with individuals in a number of communities in this country that can be helpful to us in terms of information." Hence, a similar dragnet was cast in early 2003, when, according to the Justice Department, the FBI interviewed nearly 10,000 Iraqis in the United States. These interviews, the FBI revealed, "resulted in 250 reports that provided information on possible weapons production, storage and underground facilities."

Some may wonder what the guardians of civil liberties are upset about: Why shouldn't the government interview people? The answer is that these investigations are an intrusion on thousands of people, suspected of nothing, who would rather not spend their afternoon being interrogated in an FBI office. Moreover, a Department of Justice official explained privately that anyone who declines to be interviewed or simply to show up becomes a suspect and may well be brought in for interrogation.

These are steps the United States would not take in normal times. They are a price we must pay—and not a trivial one—to minimize the likelihood of terrorist attacks in our midst.

Measures That Remain Troubling

Still other new measures raise difficult questions. Some of these policies have already been modified. Others have been abandoned. Still others, appropriate to our new security environment, should be retained but with enhanced provisions for accountability.

Military Tribunals. There is a clear need to avoid disclosing our intelligence sources and methods in open court—so much so that in several instances, an American charged with espionage has been allowed to bargain down the sentence to avoid his pleading not guilty, which would necessitate a public trial. Terrorists should not be allowed to benefit from a right to demand a public trial. Nevertheless, there did appear to be cause for concern when the White House announced in November 2001 that under some circumstances, civilians might be tried before military tribunals. The procedures to be used were left vague; the implication seemed to be that the death penalty could be imposed by a mere majority of the tribunal and that there would be no opportunity for appeal. In March 2002, however, the Pentagon clarified the matter, announcing that a unanimous verdict will be required for the death penalty, that most proceedings would be open to the press, that defendants would be eligible for military lawyers at government expense, and that suspects would be presumed innocent until proven guilty. The rules also provide for appeals through the military, specifically review by the military Court of Criminal Appeals, the Court of Appeals for Armed Forces, and the Supreme Court. These are welcome clarifications. Still, military tribunals should be used as sparingly as possible. Up to this point, their use has been avoided.

Eyes and Ears. Operation TIPS (the Terrorist Information and Prevention System) was proposed as part of Citizen Corps, the voluntary service the Bush administration introduced following the president's 2002 State of the Union address and through which Americans can help protect the homeland. TIPS, as conceived by the White House, was to serve as "a nationwide mechanism for reporting suspicious terrorist activity." Americans would report questionable activities they encountered by calling a hotline. To many, it sounded as if people were being asked to snoop on one another, as if every mailman, meter reader, and UPS driver might be peeping into one's living room and reporting whatever he deemed odd. If such a program had been implemented, it would have fueled enormous mistrust among Americans. It also would have been truly unreasonable, generating millions of false reports that would have overloaded authorities already afraid of being blamed for missing some genuine warnings of terrorist preparations.

Fortunately, TIPS, with its overtones of invasion of privacy, was killed in a little-known provision of the Homeland Security Act. It should be noted, however, that other programs continue to invite people to report suspicious activity they observe in public places. In the spring of 2003, for instance, New York City introduced the slogan "If You See Something, Say Something" to encourage people riding the subway to keep their eyes open. And New York State maintains a hotline introduced in September 2002. Such measures should be evaluated by an independent analyst to determine whether they yield sufficient leads to justify them.

New Powers: New Accountability? In addition, the government has acquired a whole slew of other new powers since the first attack on the World Trade Center in 1993. None of these is small potatoes; together they amount to a considerable shift in the balance between security and individual rights. Public debate often focuses on whether these new powers are needed. I take it for granted that they are called for, given the new level of threat; the issue is whether their application is being adequately supervised.

Fortunately, TIPS, with its overtones of invasion of privacy, was killed in a little-known provision of the Homeland Security Act.

One of these new powers, enacted in 1994 and extended in 1996, is the ability to charge someone with the crime of providing "material support" to terrorists. "Material support" is a broad category that includes money, training, expert advice or assistance, and false documents or identification. Making a donation to the Holy Land Foundation of Richardson, Texas (which claims to support charitable work but actually provides support to Palestinian terrorist groups), for instance, can land a person in jail—whether or not he knew the true purposes of the foundation.

Also, since 9/11, new "sneak and peek" legislation contained in the Patriot Act allows authorities, with a court order of course, to search a home in connection with a terrorism investigation without notifying the homeowner, as required by a normal search warrant. Under the Patriot Act (Section 215), business records and computer hard drives, including those of libraries, can also be searched, with a court order, in connection with a terrorism investigation. Furthermore, an American citizen can be declared an "enemy combatant," depriving him of many of his constitutional protections. This has happened in precisely two cases. President Bush declared José Padilla, suspected of planning a "dirty bomb" attack with Al Qaeda, an enemy combatant. Yaser Hamdi, who was born in the United States, but spent most of his life in Saudi Arabia, was captured on the battlefield in Afghanistan.

Critics view these new powers as threatening our democracy. As I see it, these powers are neither dangerous nor reasonable per se, but dangerous if employed without close scrutiny, and reasonable if properly supervised.

Some oversight is built into the structure of federal agencies, including law enforcement: Supervisors are supposed to watch what their subordinates do, and Congress is meant to provide another layer of oversight. Then there are the courts. It is encouraging that those new security measures that have been reviewed by appeals courts have, by and large, been upheld. Another source of accountability is the inspector general of the Justice Department. Indeed, last month he issued a report that criticized the ways the FBI dealt with some of those detained on immigration offenses in the months after the terrorist attack. Nevertheless, even this multilayered set of safeguards is by no means foolproof—as we were reminded by the FBI scandals in Boston, where agents protected mob informants in the 1990s and warned a mob boss that he was about to be arrested; he is still on the lam.

These [new government] powers are dangerous if employed without close scrutiny, and reasonable if properly supervised.

The good news is that some new measures of accountability have been put in place alongside the new powers. Thus, the Homeland Security Act of 2002 provides for an officer whose job it is to protect privacy and another whose job is to promote civil rights and liberties. It is too soon to tell how effective these officers will be. Either way, I believe Americans would welcome heightened scrutiny of the way these powers are exercised.

Further, accountability might take the form of review by a panel of judges similar to the FISA court. Such a panel could regularly examine the cases of Americans charged under the new powers. It could meet in closed session and release its findings to the public in summary form. For instance, it might report that, say, suspects were held appropriately in 80 percent of the cases under review; in another 15 percent of cases, more information was needed (bureaucratese for "We have doubts about some aspect of these cases"); and in the remaining 5 percent, the detainee must be released forthwith. I focus on Americans because noncitizens have fewer rights than members of our national community. Which rights noncitizens are entitled to and how those rights are to be safeguarded requires a separate examination.

Problems Not Yet Addressed

Many provisions of the Patriot Act expire in 2005. Some of them the Justice Department and Congress are seeking to extend one at a time. For instance, in May, the Senate passed what is called the

"Moussaoui-fix" bill, which would allow law enforcement to conduct surveillance of "lone wolf" terrorist suspects. (Currently, association with a known terrorist organization must be documented.)

Another safety measure deserves the attention of Congress: more reliable means of personal identification. The usefulness of watch lists, airline passenger profiles, student tracking systems, and dossiers on suspects is greatly impaired as long as people can readily obtain false identification (typically driver's licenses) or steal someone else's identity.

This is no small matter. Driver's licenses are a de facto national ID card. Although they are issued by states, each state honors all the others'. People are regularly required to present their license (or some other document, such as a green card) when they fly, drive, or enter numerous public buildings and quite a few private ones. Whatever loss of anonymity and privacy is involved, law-abiding Americans have already suffered it. But as long as terrorists and other criminals can readily obtain false or fraudulent driver's licenses, many new security measures are undermined. Hence, we need to make driver's licenses meet a basic standard of reliability, as the American Association of Motor Vehicle Administrators has recommended. Bipartisan bills to this effect were introduced in the 107th Congress—one by representatives James Moran and Tom Davis, the other by senators Dick Durbin and John McCain—but garnered little support. The administration should back the effort to make driver's licenses tamperproof and uniform across the 50 states.

The world has changed, and we cannot afford to pretend that any recalibration of our rights in view of our new need to defend the United States at home amounts to an attack on the Constitution. This is not to say that we should mindlessly consent to any innovation introduced in the name of safety. Societies have no precise control mechanisms; they tend to oversteer. Hence, significant corrections in the delicate balance between public safety and individual rights typically require their own corrections. After 9/11, there were good reasons to rush through legislation expanding government authority, given the fear of imminent follow-up attacks by sleeper cells. Now is the time to revise and fine-tune these measures.

When all is said and done, most of the measures that the Bush administration has launched since 9/11 are reasonable and necessary. Others may well be necessary, but call for close supervision by Congress to ensure that the government does not yield to new temptations. Regrettably, there still are some pressing security needs, above all in our ability to reliably identify people, and in that area the government needs more, not less, authority.

At War with Liberty

By Stephen J. Schulhofer
The American Prospect, March 2003

As expected, September 11 has prompted an expansion of law-enforcement powers at almost every level. And who would have it otherwise? For those of us who live and work in Manhattan, 9-11 was not a single horrific day but an extended nightmare. For weeks, kiosks, store windows, and parks displayed fliers by the thousands, pleading for information about loved ones still missing. National Guard units seemed to be everywhere. Day after day, the air—gray and acrid—carried the smell of burning flesh.

No, the "war" metaphor is not just convenient political spin. And despite shameless hyping of "sleeper cells" and color-coded threat levels, no responsible person can dismiss the danger of devastating future attacks. Actions to strengthen law enforcement are not simply the product of panic or paranoia.

But the particulars are troubling, and worse. Predictably, there has been overreaction and political grandstanding. More surprising is the neglect. The administration has inexcusably swept aside urgent security needs while it continues to win public acclaim for toughness by targeting and scapegoating civil liberties.

An accounting of the state of our liberties should begin with the positives. To his credit, the president has preached tolerance and respect for our Muslim neighbors. Unlike previous wartime governments, his administration has not sought to prosecute dissenters for political speech, has not attempted anything comparable to the internment of Japanese Americans during World War II and (technically, at least) has not tried to suspend the writ of habeas corpus.

But to measure performance by these standards is to set the bar terribly low; these were sorry historical embarrassments. And 9-11 has already produced several comparable missteps. The administration's efforts to stymie habeas corpus rival the civil-liberties low points of prior wars, as does Bush's determination (wholly without precedent) to hold American citizens indefinitely on disputed charges without affording them a trial in *any* forum, civil or military. Also without precedent are the oddly imbalanced means chosen to fight this battle. Never before in American history has an administration stinted on many homeland- and national-security expenditures and made tax cuts its top priority at a time of war.

Conventional wisdom about striking a balance between liberty and security obscures the fact that responses to 9-11 are deeply flawed from *both* perspectives.

Surveillance and Privacy

The USA PATRIOT Act, passed in October 2001, expanded government surveillance powers in multiple directions. Investigators won new authority to track Internet use and to obtain previously confidential business and educational records. Prosecutors gained access to the broad search and wiretap powers of the Foreign Intelligence Surveillance Act. The Department of the Treasury expanded its authority to require banks, brokers, and other businesses to report cash transactions and "suspicious activities," which include any transaction that differs from ones the customer typically conducts. Though the Department of Justice created a furor with its proposal to encourage voluntary snooping by private citizens, the Treasury Department regulations *require* private citizens and businesses to become eyes and ears for the government.

Many Americans are ready to sacrifice these sorts of privacies to obtain any nugget of information about Al Qaeda plans. Nonethe-

---

The rollback of privacy rights has three flaws that should trouble us all.

---

less, the rollback of privacy rights has three flaws that should trouble us all. First, worries about terrorism provide no reason to expand law-enforcement power across the board. Yet FBI and Treasury Department agents can use most of their new powers to investigate allegations of prostitution, gambling, insider trading, or any other offense. There is no excuse for exploiting 9-11 to intrude on privacy in pursuit of these unrelated goals.

Second, accountability measures, though neglected in the rush to pass the PATRIOT Act, need not impair the usefulness of the new powers but, if well designed, would actually enhance them. The FBI's "Carnivore" system for spying on e-mail, for example, desperately needs procedures to preserve audit trails and ensure the accountability of agents who have access to it.

Finally, additional information is useless unless our agencies are able to make sense of it. It's now well known that before 9-11, the FBI and the CIA had important clues about the plot in hand, but as one FBI agent put it, "We didn't know what we knew." Because a large part of what we lack is not raw data but the ability to separate significant intelligence from "noise," pulling more information into government files may aggravate rather than solve the problem. Even before 9-11, Treasury Department officials complained that the staggering volume of reports they received—more than a million every month—was interfering with enforcement. Absent a substantial infusion of resources (which the administration has failed to provide), powerful new surveillance tools can give us only a false sense of comfort.

Unleashing the FBI

Last May headlines featured for days the startling news that in July and August 2001, agents in Minneapolis and Phoenix, Ariz., had urged investigations of Zacarias Moussaoui and the flight schools, only to be stifled by FBI headquarters—an enormous blunder. In response, Attorney General John Ashcroft called a press conference to denounce "bureaucratic restrictions" that were preventing FBI agents from doing their jobs.

The rules he had in mind grew out of extensive FBI abuses in the 1950s and 1960s. Free to pursue random tips and their own hunches, agents back then intimidated dissidents, damaged reputations, and produced thousands of dossiers on public figures, private citizens, political parties, and social movements. By 1975, FBI headquarters held more than half a million domestic intelligence files.

Such sprawling dragnets are as inefficient as they are abusive. Rules to rein them in were adopted in 1976 by President Gerald Ford and have been reaffirmed by every president since. Nonetheless, Ashcroft ridiculed these guidelines as absurdly restrictive. He said—incorrectly—that the rules barred FBI agents from surfing the Internet and even from observing activities in public places. He announced that he was solving this problem by allowing FBI agents to operate with much less supervision.

The civil-liberties community responded with outrage. But far from hurting Ashcroft's popularity, the criticism reinforced his intended message: that defendants' rights had hobbled law enforcement. The failure to pursue the flight-school leads was in effect blamed on the American Civil Liberties Union, and the Justice Department presented itself as taking firm, corrective action.

What actually occurred was rather different. One set of guidelines the attorney general relaxed governs investigations of "general crimes"—gambling, theft, and other offenses *not* related to terrorism. The other guidelines he loosened govern investigations of *domestic* terrorist groups. Unnoticed in the brouhaha, the rules governing international terrorism cases—the ones that apply to Al Qaeda—weren't affected by the changes at all.

Behind the screen of this public-relations maneuver, damage was inflicted in several directions. Public frustration with central oversight was understandable under the circumstances, but none of the guidelines, even the more restrictive domestic regimes, impeded the kinds of investigative steps the Minneapolis and Phoenix agents had urged. What the field offices needed was better supervision, not less of it. Yet Ashcroft's actions obscured responsibility for FBI missteps, and instead of censure, the FBI was rewarded with greater discretion. As in the case of the PATRIOT Act, fear of terrorism offered an occasion for bait and switch: The guideline revisions don't in any way address the Al Qaeda threat that preoccupies the public, yet they leave us with heightened risks to civil liberties and much less effective management at the FBI.

> *Secrecy, Ashcroft stated, is necessary to protect the privacy of detainees.*

Detentions and Secrecy

In the months following 9-11, federal agents arrested approximately 1,200 foreign nationals. Hundreds—the precise number is unknown—were held for months before being cleared and released; others remain in detention, ostensibly awaiting deportation. Courts are still sorting through the many issues the detentions pose.

Particularly troubling is the extraordinary secrecy surrounding these sweeps. The government has refused to release the names of any of the detainees. Individuals charged and afforded immigration hearings find those hearings closed to the press and even to their own families.

The government's justifications for secrecy are revealing. Secrecy, Ashcroft stated, is necessary to protect the privacy of detainees. Because many of them desperately wanted their names made public—so that aid organizations and lawyers could contact them—and because the Justice Department could have afforded secrecy to detainees who requested it, the privacy claim was painfully disingenuous. In litigation, Justice Department lawyers added the argument that releasing the names of terrorists would give the terrorists' cohorts clues about the progress of the investigation. This "roadmap" argument, though not entirely frivolous, is embarrassingly thin. Because all detainees have the right to make phone calls, and because gag orders have not been imposed on their lawyers and family, detainees who really are terrorists can easily signal their confederates.

Secrecy across the board, without any obligation to present case-specific reasons for it in court, has less to do with the war on terrorism than with the administration's consistent efforts, firmly in place before 9-11, to insulate executive action from public scrutiny. The cumulative effect of these efforts is an unprecedented degree of power—an attempt simultaneously to cut off the right to counsel or judicial review and any ability of the press to report what happens to individuals arrested on U.S. soil.

The Assault on Habeas Corpus

José Padilla, the so-called dirty bomber who allegedly planned to explode a bomb laced with radioactive material, was arrested in May 2002 at Chicago's O'Hare Airport and held for a month as a material witness. Counsel was appointed for him, and he was due to be brought to court on June 11. Instead, two nights before that date,

President Bush decided that Padilla was an "enemy combatant," a finding that the Justice Department tenaciously argues cannot be reviewed by any federal judge.

That night, without notice to his court-appointed counsel, Padilla was taken from federal detention in Manhattan, put on a military plane bound for South Carolina, and thrown into a Navy brig. That was June 9, and Padilla hasn't been heard from since. The government has refused to let him speak to the press or to his own attorney, and has done everything in its power to deny him access to the courts.

Enemy infiltrators have posed acute threats to public safety before, notably during the Civil War. Lincoln, a straightforward man, responded by suspending the writ of habeas corpus.

That is not the Bush administration style. When Padilla's lawyer, Donna Newman, tried to file a habeas petition on her client's behalf, the government suggested no need to suspend the writ. Its argument was the "narrow" one that the Padilla petition was invalid because he hadn't signed it. Having deliberately blocked all contact between Padilla and the outside world, the government told the court that a valid habeas petition required his signature, that Newman couldn't sign for him (how do we know that Padilla still wanted her to obtain his release?), and that his own lawyer had no standing to ask the court's help because she had no "significant relationship" with him. Federal Judge Michael Mukasey ultimately dismissed these arguments as frivolous. He ruled that Newman had to be granted access to her client and that he would review the "enemy combatant" designation to be sure it was supported by "some evidence."

Mukasey's decision was announced on Dec. 9, yet Padilla remains incommunicado. As of early February, the government was continuing to find new reasons why Newman should be denied all contact with him, though Judge Mukasey, losing patience, probably will insist that a visit be permitted soon. After eight months (and counting), Padilla will eventually get to see his lawyer, and the judge will decide whether "some evidence" supports the detention.

The New York Times and *The Washington Post* praised Mukasey for his courage in standing up to the government. But we should take little comfort from his decision. Detention (incommunicado, to boot) has continued for more than eight months without any judicial review. Normally, detention without a hearing becomes unconstitutional after 48 hours.

More important, what's left of the writ of habeas corpus? Paradoxically, Padilla was lucky because the administration initially treated him as a material witness and a judge appointed counsel for him. Next time the government will just send the detainee straight to the Navy, without stopping first in a federal court. The Navy won't let him communicate with anyone in the outside world, and there won't be any Donna Newman to file a habeas petition for him. The only way to get a case like that before a judge would be for a family member to claim standing. That should work, though this Justice Department seems seriously capable of litigating whether a detainee has a "significant relationship" with his mother. There is also a less technical problem: the secrecy policy. If the government detains someone who isn't regularly in touch with his mother, she may not know that he has been locked away indefinitely in a Navy brig.

The other worry in Mukasey's decision, for any case that gets to court, is the standard of review: "some evidence." The charge against Padilla is based on a Pentagon affidavit reporting tips from unidentified informants who are unavailable for cross-examination. That's obviously not proof beyond a reasonable doubt. It's not even probable cause sufficient to support a routine wiretap, as the affidavit gives no basis for assessing the informants' reliability. But there is *some* evidence.

If the Supreme Court upholds the "some evidence" standard, it won't matter whether detainees get to file habeas petitions. An unsupported tip from a confidential source is still some evidence, and that will be all it takes to require deference to a president's finding. That finding of enemy combatant status, in turn, is enough in the administration's view to support detention for the duration of this conflict, without any trial at all.

The government says its approach is rooted in its need to continue incommunicado interrogation, for an indefinite period, in order to find out what Padilla knows. If he hasn't talked at this point, after eight months of interrogation, it's hard to believe another eight or 10 months will do the trick, or that whatever Padilla knows isn't stale. But we can't rule out the possibility that after many months (or years) of isolation, a suspect might eventually reveal something useful.

The problem with that argument is the Constitution—not just its fine points but the very idea of a government under law. If the mere possibility of a useful interrogation is enough to support indefinite detention incommunicado, no rights and no checks and balances are available at all, except when the executive chooses to grant them. If a ruler in any other country claimed unilateral powers of this sort, Americans would be quick to recognize the affront to the most basic of human rights.

Nonetheless, the government relies on two lines of precedent to support its approach. First is *Ex Parte Quirin*, the German saboteurs case. In World War II, eight German naval officers, one of whom claimed to be a U.S. citizen, landed secretly in the United States and were arrested. After trial by a military tribunal, seven were executed. The Supreme Court held that because they were members of the enemy armed forces, the military had jurisdiction (as it did over members of our own armed forces) to try them. The Court said that military jurisdiction was permissible because the defendants were "admitted enemy invaders."

In the media and in court, the Bush administration argues that *Quirin* squarely settles its power over Padilla. The administration is right only if there is no important difference between being an admitted enemy and being an accused enemy. The argument boils down to the claim that because a person who admits guilt can be punished, the law should allow the same result when the president reviews a secret record and finds the crucial facts in the privacy of the Oval Office.

The government's other precedents are the cases holding that on the battlefield, military discretion is unquestioned. And in this war on terrorism, it says, the entire nation is a battlefield. That analogy isn't completely false, but if the military can do within the United States whatever it could do in Afghanistan, again, checks and balances are over for the duration.

The American homeland has been threatened before. The Civil War brought four years of fighting on American soil, and Hawaii was a theater of active military operations throughout World War II. In both situations, the military argued the need for displacing civilian courts, and in both situations, the Supreme Court rejected the argument explicitly. "Martial law," the Court said in *Ex Parte Milligan*, "cannot arise from a threatened invasion. The necessity must be actual and present . . . such as effectually closes the courts. . . . If martial law is continued after the courts are reinstated, it is a gross usurpation of power."

The presumption against military detention, whenever civilian courts are functioning, is not merely a doctrinal technicality. The central premise of government under law is that executive officials, no matter how well intentioned, cannot be allowed unreviewable power to imprison a citizen. Even in times of dire emergency, the Supreme Court has been consistent and emphatic on this point.

"Fiscal Restraint"

While aggressively eroding civil liberties, the Bush administration has neglected many obvious security priorities. An essential first step in a serious counterterrorism effort is to determine what mistakes we made before 9-11. President Roosevelt ordered an independent inquiry less than three weeks after Pearl Harbor. NASA acted within hours to order an independent inquiry into the *Columbia* space shuttle disaster. Yet it's now more than a year since 9-11, and an independent inquiry into what went wrong is just getting started.

Last September, after opposing such an inquiry for months, Bush made a high-visibility announcement supporting a 9-11 investigation. But he then quietly torpedoed a bipartisan congressional agreement on its structure. That issue wasn't resolved until December, so the inquiry is just beginning to staff up. And with a budget that cannot exceed $3 million, its prospects are not auspicious. By comparison, to unearth every detail concerning Whitewater, Monica Lewinsky, and other President Clinton matters, Congress gave Independent Counsel Kenneth Starr 20 times more money, a total of $70 million.

Other expenditure decisions are even more scandalous. Last year Congress appropriated $419 million for enhanced airport security, $82 million for upgrading FBI counterterrorism technology, $39 million for inspecting cargo containers at our ports, and $165 million for protecting the food and water supply. But in August, President Bush froze all these funds, stressing the need to exercise "fiscal restraint." The National Nuclear Security Administration, the agency that protects our nuclear stockpile and our weapons laboratories, is now struggling with a shortage of security guards. Yet, incredibly, the agency was forced to announce a hiring freeze last November because of budget constraints. Though we now may be just weeks away from a new war that will put our homeland at great risk, counterterrorism efforts such as these have been on hold since last August.

There is a startling disconnect here. The rhetoric of war and national emergency is invoked over and over to support limits on civil liberties, but when the subject is tax cuts, talk of a national emergency stops. The administration's strategy is not captured by the cliché about "shifting the balance" from liberty to security because it is shortchanging us on both.

The White House does not exaggerate when it talks about the dangers of Al Qaeda and the need for a "war" on terrorism. Precisely because the risks of a terrorist attack are so serious, administration policies should be troubling to every American. The decision to blame civil liberties and to draw attention away from other aspects of an effective counterterrorism strategy is a dangerous choice.

Acts of Resistance

By Elaine Scarry
Harper's Magazine, May 2004

When the U.S.A. Patriot Act arrived in our midst in the fall of 2001, its very title seemed to deliver an injury: "Uniting and Strengthening America by Providing Appropriate Tools Required to Intercept and Obstruct Terrorism." One might have thought that "United States of America" would be a sufficient referent for the letters "U.S.A." and that no one would presume to bestow a new meaning on the word "patriot," with its heavy freight of history (Paul Revere, Patrick Henry, Emma Lazarus) and its always fresh aspiration ("O beautiful for patriot dream").

In the two and a half years since it was passed, the U.S.A. Patriot Act has become the locus of resistance against the unceasing injuries of the Bush-Rumsfeld-Ashcroft triumvirate, as first one community, then two, then 11, then 27, and now 272 have passed resolutions against it, as have four state legislatures. The letters "U.S.A." and the word "patriot" are gradually reacquiring their earlier solidity and sufficiency as local and state governments reanimate the practice of self-rule by opposing the Patriot Act's assault on the personal privacy, free flow of information, and freedom of association that lie at the heart of democracy. Each of the resolutions affirms the town's obligation to uphold the constitutional rights of all persons who live there, and many of them explicitly direct police and other residents to refrain from carrying out the provisions of the Act, even when instructed to do so by a federal officer.

When the resistance was first beginning, in the winter of 2001–2002, it took five months for the first five resolutions to come into being; by the winter of 2003–2004, a new resolution was being drafted almost every day. The resolutions come from towns ranging from small villages—Wendell, Massachusetts (986), Riverside, Washington (348), Gaston, Oregon (620)—to huge cities—Philadelphia (1,517,550), Baltimore (651,000), Chicago (2,896,000), Detroit (951,000), Austin (656,300), San Francisco (777,000). Approximately a third of the resolutions come from towns and cities with populations between 20,000 and 200,000.

The fact that the Patriot Act has engendered such resistance may at first seem puzzling. True, its legislative history is sordid: it was rushed through Congress in several days; no hearings were held; it went largely unread; only a few of its many egregious provisions were modified. But at least it *was* passed by Congress: many other blows to civil liberties have been delivered as unmodified executive edicts, such as the formation of military tribunals and the nullification of attorney-client privilege. True, the Patriot Act severed words from their meanings (beginning with the letters "U.S.A."), but executive statements associating Iraq with nuclear weapons and with Al Qaeda severed words from their basis in material fact, at the very great cost of a war that continues to be materially and mortally destructive. True, the Patriot Act has degraded the legal stature of the United States by permitting the executive branch to bypass constitutional law, but our legal degradation outside the Patriot Act has gone even further: Evidence indicates that the Bush Administration has created offshore torture centers in Bagram, Afghanistan, and on the British island of Diego Garcia, and has sent prisoners to interrogation centers in countries with documented histories of torture such as Egypt, Jordan, Saudi Arabia, and Syria.

The executive edicts, the war against Iraq, and the alleged use of torture have all elicited protest, but what differentiates the opposition to the Patriot Act is the fact that it has enabled the population to move beyond vocalizing dissent to retarding, and potentially reversing, the executive's inclination to carry out actions divorced from the will of the people.

If many members of Congress failed to read the Patriot Act during its swift passage, it is in part because it is almost unreadable. The Patriot Act is written as an extended sequence of additions to and deletions from previously existing statutes, instructing the bewildered reader to insert three words into paragraph X of statute Y without ever providing the altered sentence in either its original or its amended form. Only someone who had scores of earlier statutes open to the relevant pages could step painstakingly through the revisions. Reading the Patriot Act is like standing outside the public library trying to infer the sentences in the books inside by listening to hundreds of mice chewing away on the pages.

The Act does, however, have a coherent and unitary purpose: to increase the power of the Justice Department and to decrease the rights of individual persons. The constitutional rights abridged by the Patriot Act are enumerated in the town resolutions, which most often specify violations of the First Amendment guarantee of free speech and assembly, the Fourth Amendment guarantee against search and seizure, the Fifth and Fourteenth Amendment guarantees of due process, and the Sixth and Eighth Amendment guarantees of a speedy and public trial and of protection against cruel and unusual punishment.

The objective of the Patriot Act becomes even clearer if it is understood concretely as making the population visible and the Justice Department invisible. The Act inverts the constitutional requirement that people's lives be private and the work of government officials be public; it instead crafts a set of conditions that make our inner lives transparent and the workings of the government opaque. Either one of these outcomes would imperil democracy; together they not only injure the country but also cut off the avenues of repair.

When we say democracy requires that the people's privacy be ensured, we mean that we ourselves should control the degree to which, and the people to whom, our lives are revealed. Under the Patriot Act, the inner lives of people are made involuntarily transparent by provisions that increase the ability of federal officers to enter and search a person's house, to survey private medical records, business records, library records, and educational records, and to monitor telephone, email, and Internet use. The Fourth Amendment states: "The right of the people to be secure in their persons, houses, papers, and effects, against unreasonable searches and seizures, shall not be violated, and no Warrants shall issue, *but upon probable cause,* supported by Oath or affirmation, and *particularly describing the place to be searched, and the persons or things to be seized*" (emphasis added). The Patriot Act both explicitly lowers the "probable cause" requirement, thereby diminishing judicial review, and eliminates the specificity clause—"particularly describing the place to be searched, and the persons or things to be seized"—which, like "probable cause," puts severe restraints on the scope and duration of the search. The Act is a sweeping license to search and seize, everywhere and anywhere, guided not by court-validated standards of evidence but by Justice Department hunches and racially inflected intuitions.

> *Under the Patriot Act, the inner lives of people are made involuntarily transparent.*

As necessary to democracy as the nontransparency of persons is the transparency of government actions, and indeed the Constitution pauses again and again to insist upon open records: "Each house [of Congress] shall keep a Journal of its Proceedings, and from time to time publish the same" with "the Yeas and Nays of the Members . . . entered on the Journal"; "a regular Statement and Account of the Receipts and Expenditures of all public Money shall be published from time to time"; presidential objections to a piece of legislation must be forwarded to the house in which the legislation originated and published in its journal; the counting of the Electoral College votes must take place in the presence of the full Congress; treason proceedings will take place in "open Court" and criminal prosecutions in a "public trial," etc.

The obligation of each branch to make its actions public—to make them visible both to the people and to the other branches—is often construed as a right belonging to the populace, the right of "freedom of information." Indeed, it is hard to disagree with the argument that democratic deliberation is impossible without this access to information. Secrecy, the legal theorist Cass Sunstein writes, "is inconsistent with the principle of self-rule." He identifies citizen deliberation as the primary benefit of open government, but there are other benefits, including checks and balances (one branch cannot check the other if it does not know what the other is doing), and "sunlight as a disinfectant" (if deliberations are carried out in secret, "participants may be less careful to ensure that their behavior is unaffected by illegitimate or irrelevant considerations").

Because both the privacy of individual action and the publication of government action are necessary to democratic self-rule, the major complaint of the local resolutions has been the damage done to the liberties of persons and to the integrity of our laws. The most forceful formulation of this worry comes at the conclusion of the Blount County, Tennessee, resolution, which calls upon all residents "to study the Bill of Rights so that they can recognize and resist attempts to undermine our Constitutional Republic . . . and declare null and void all future attempts to establish Martial Law, [or] Declared States of Emergency." Although most of the other resolutions are more measured in their language, they consistently register the view that both the people and the laws of this country are endangered.

The resolutions have a second, closely related focus. Although the Patriot Act enables the federal government to detain and investigate both citizens and non-citizens, and to carry out surveillance of both citizens and non-citizens, its blows fall most heavily on those who are not U.S. citizens.

Consider section 412. As summarized by the city of Ann Arbor, Michigan, it permits the incarceration of non-citizens for seven days without charge and "for six month periods indefinitely, without access to counsel" if the attorney general "determines release would endanger the security of the country or of a specific person." Before it was modified by Congress, the bill authorized the unlimited detention of immigrants, but the revision is less of an improvement than it seems, since various loopholes release the executive branch from the seven-day constraint.

The resolutions collectively work to prevent this imperilment of all residents of the United States. Almost without exception, the 272 resolutions celebrate their commitment to law and liberty for all "persons" or "residents," not only "citizens." This is expressed in part as a matter of constitutional conviction: The very first clause of the very first resolution (Ann Arbor) begins by echoing the 2001 Supreme Court decision *Zadvydas v. Davis*: "The due process and equal protection clauses of the 5th and 14th Amendments to the United States Constitution guarantee certain due process and equal protection rights to all residents of the United States regardless of citizenship or immigration status." Other resolutions remind all residents that discrimination based on "citizenship status" is no more permissible than discrimination based on race or gender. They complain that the Patriot Act tries "to drive a wedge" between citizens and non-citizens, or between police and foreign nationals, a situation held to be intolerable because the town depends on the diversity of its population for its "vitality" and its "economy, culture, and civic character."

Almost the only time when "citizens" are singled out is when the documents place on them the burden of acting to ensure that all "persons" or "residents" enjoy the benefits of due process, protection from unwarranted search and seizure, freedom of speech, freedom of assembly, and privacy. If, in other words, citizens are unique, it is because they are the guardians of rights belonging to citizens and non-citizens alike, not the exclusive holders of those rights.

In addition to aiming blows at our legal framework of self-governance, the Patriot Act licenses the executive branch to harm other institutions—among them, financial markets and universities—and once again its blows appear to be structural.

Take, for example, the provisions that require bankers, broker-dealers, and trading advisers to file "suspicious activity reports" (SARs) when they notice their clients carrying out

---

Universities . . . are among the institutions the Patriot Act seeks to change.

---

unusual transfers greater than $5,000. Failure to file is punishable by criminal and civil charges, with fines reaching $10,000. Furthermore, they are prohibited from telling their client about the SAR, which not only taints the client relationship but eliminates at the outset the possibility of determining whether the transfer has some sensible explanation that, if they only knew it, would convince them that the filing was preposterous.

Universities, too, are among the institutions the Patriot Act seeks to change, and the situation may be swiftly assessed by looking at the most widely discussed aspect of the Act, section 215, which applies to both college and public libraries (and, in many cases, bookstores). When approached by an FBI or CIA agent, librarians must turn over a record of the books a specified patron has taken out, and, like the bankers, they are prohibited from telling anyone of the intelligence gathering in which they have just participated.

In his fall 2003 tour of 30 cities to defend the Patriot Act, Attorney General John Ashcroft dismissed the idea that the Justice Department could conceivably care about librarians or library records. A University of Illinois study found, however, that by February 2002 (four months after the Patriot Act was passed) 4 percent of all U.S. libraries and 11 percent of libraries in communities of more than 50,000 people had already been visited by FBI agents requesting information about their patrons' reading habits. Ashcroft insisted that not-yet-released FBI records would demonstrate the indifference of the Justice Department to the libraries, but the

Justice Department has in fact refused to release these very same records, despite Freedom of Information Act petitions filed by the American Civil Liberties Union and other organizations.

In distilled form, the logic of the Patriot Act and its defense involves four steps: Maximize the power of the Justice Department; erase the public record of Justice Department actions; respond with indignation if anyone protests that the Justice Department might actually be using its newly expanded powers; point out that the protesters are speaking without any hard evidence or facts without mentioning that the executive branch has withheld those very facts from the public.

From the founding of this country the phrase "a government of laws and not of men" has meant that the country cannot pass open-ended laws that will be good if the governors happen to be good and bad if the governors happen to be bad. The goal has always been to pass laws that will protect everyone regardless of the temperament and moral character of the individual governors. The country, as Justice Davis famously observed in the 19th century, "has no right to expect that it will always have wise and humane rulers." That's why it is crucial to pass good laws. And crucial, also, to repeal bad ones.

Despite impediments to resistance, 272 towns, cities, and counties have created a firewall against executive trespass in their communities. The resolutions direct residents to decline to assist the federal government in any act that violates the Constitution: local police should abstain from assisting federal officers in house searches that violate the Fourth Amendment, and librarians should abstain from giving out private library records that violate the First and Fourth Amendments.

Here we have the key to why the Patriot Act—rather than the executive edicts—has become the focus of so much resistance. Since military tribunals do not require the assistance of the population, what we think about the military tribunals is a matter of indifference to the executive. Since the country has a standing army rather than a draft, the war against Iraq was neither ours to assist nor ours to decline to assist. If, without the population's assistance, 5,000 foreign nationals can be detained without charges (only three of whom were ever charged with terrorism-related acts), then the population's disapproval of this detention is like smoke rings in the wind. But since the aspirations encoded in the Patriot Act cannot come about without the help of police, bankers, and librarians, the refusal to assist provides a concrete brake on the actions of the federal government.

Although the Justice Department has tried to portray resistance to the Patriot Act as a liberal complaint, the resisters repeatedly assert that they occupy positions across the political spectrum. And, so far, both Congress and the courts appear to be listening. Various congressmen and senators have initiated bills to nullify or limit specific provisions of the Patriot Act. In July 2003 the House passed an amendment to the 2004 Appropriations Bill that withholds all federal funding from section 213—the provision that allows the Justice Department to search a house without notifying the resident. The courts, too, share the concerns of the local resolutions. In January a federal court in Los Angeles ruled one section of the Patriot Act unconstitutional: the judge objected to the provision making it a crime to provide "expert advice or assistance" to terrorists on the grounds that the phrasing is so vague as to license the Justice Department to interfere with First Amendment speech guarantees. In December two federal courts issued rulings declaring acts of detention carried out by the Bush Administration unlawful on grounds similar to those mentioned in the town resolutions.

Sorting out the legal status of the Patriot Act may take some time. The United States Constitution prohibits acts that the Patriot Act licenses, and, although constitutional provisions take legal precedence over contradictory legislation, for the time being the Act appears to empower the federal government not only to call upon the country's residents for assistance but also to impose criminal and civil penalties on those who fail to assist.

Whether the resistance to the Patriot Act gains momentum or is ultimately derailed, the town resolutions remind us that the power of enforcement lies not just with local police but with all those who reside in cities, towns, villages, isolated byways, and country lanes. Law—whether local, state, federal, or constitutional—is only real if, as Patrick Henry said, the rest of us will put our hands to it, put our hearts to it, stand behind it.

II. Racial Profiling:
Narrowing the Pool or
Pooling Narrowly?

Editor's Introduction

Racial profiling is the use of racial or ethnic criteria by law-enforcement officials to single out individuals for differential treatment or investigation. Civil rights advocates have long challenged the ethics and efficacy of the procedure at a local level, but it is only in connection with the federal government's recent campaign against terror that profiling has emerged as one of the most controversial aspects of national law enforcement. On the one hand, opposers of profiling argue that using race or ethnicity as a way of narrowing a pool of potential suspects is both discriminatory and ineffective. On the other hand, supporters of profiling as an antiterrorism tactic maintain that it would be a waste of time and energy to screen members of all demographic groups with the same frequency and degree of caution that one would use with individuals who match the "typical" demographic profile of a terrorist. Given these competing concerns and viewpoints, what is the most appropriate and efficient way for authorities to find and arrest people who pose threats to national security? Is racial profiling a justifiable strategy that makes it easier for federal agents to track down terrorists, or is it a form of racism that risks stereotyping all young Arab men as criminals?

In "Bush Issues Racial Profiling Ban but Exempts Security Inquiries," from the *New York Times*, Eric Lichtblau reports on President Bush's issuance, in 2003, of a series of guidelines for federal agencies on the subject of profiling. Although the policy stipulates that profiling should not be used in connection with routine investigations, it contains provisions that allow for the use of race and ethnicity to identify suspects in cases related to preventing terrorism and investigating potential threats to national security. The cases for and against racial and ethnic profiling as a law-enforcement strategy are outlined in a pair of articles originally published in the *International Social Science Review*. In "Point: The Case for Profiling," Sharon R. Reddick argues that the extreme threat to national security posed by Muslim terrorists makes it necessary for federal agents to take the race of potential suspects into account when determining whether to investigate them. While Reddick concedes that profiling can be harmful when taken to extremes, she maintains that it is an expedient way to track down hijackers and other terrorists.

In "Counterpoint: The Case Against Profiling," Christina Fauchon presents a perspective contradictory to Reddick's, claiming that racial profiling is a fundamentally unethical practice that should not be used by law enforcers under any circumstances. Citing such past abuses of profiling tactics as the internment of Japanese Americans during World War II, she argues that profiling violates the constitutional right of all U.S. citizens to equal protection under the law. Furthermore, she maintains that physical appearance is a much less effective indicator of violent aims than is suspicious behavior.

In "Undermining Antiterrorism," first published in *America*, Donald Kerwin discusses the U.S. government's recent crackdown on immigration offenses, arguing that measures to weed out terrorists by targeting immigrant communities have, ironically, undermined antiterror strategy. According to Kerwin, recent instances of preemptive arrest and detention have led many immigants to regard the "war on terror" as a pretext for persecuting immigrants and punishing immigration violations; this fact has rendered them much less willing to cooperate with federal agents searching for terrorists. Furthermore, while the Bush administration has portrayed its antiterrorism plan as an attempt to protect liberty, Kerwin writes, civil libertarians claim that it has dishonored the Constitution.

Lastly, in "Straighten Up and Fly Right," from the *Wall Street Journal*, Heather Mac Donald argues that the "blind antidiscrimination reflex" of many outspoken left-wingers has handicapped antiterrorism efforts by allowing political correctness to stand in the way of appropriate security measures. According to Mac Donald, "common sense alone should determine security decisions"—even if civil libertarians regard some of the procedures deemed "common sense" by law-enforcement agents as intrusions on basic civil rights and liberties.

Bush Issues Racial Profiling Ban but Exempts Security Inquiries

BY ERIC LICHTBLAU
THE NEW YORK TIMES, JUNE 18, 2003

President Bush issued guidelines today barring federal agents from using race or ethnicity in their routine investigations, but the policy carves out clear exemptions for investigations involving terrorism and national security matters.

The new policy, representing the first time that the federal government has imposed across the board guidelines on racial profiling, governs the conduct of 70 federal law enforcement agencies. A narcotics agent, for instance, cannot focus on a specific neighborhood simply because of its racial makeup, the policy states.

In national security operations, however, the policy allows agents to use race and ethnicity in "narrow" circumstances to help "identify terrorist threats and stop potential catastrophic attacks," officials said.

Immigration officials, for instance, will continue to be able to require visitors from largely Middle Eastern countries to register with the government.

And if intelligence officials had information indicating that terrorists of a certain ethnic group planned to hijack a plane next week in California, the authorities could impose "heightened scrutiny" on men of that ethnicity who boarded planes in that area, officials said.

Arab-American and civil rights groups said the exemptions in the White House policy would give the authorities legal justification to single out Middle Easterners and others who may fall under suspicion, and they questioned whether the new policy—issued as "guidance"—would be aggressively enforced.

"This policy acknowledges racial profiling as a national concern, but it does nothing to stop it," Laura Murphy, director of the Washington office of the American Civil Liberties Union, said in an interview. "It's largely a rhetorical statement. The administration is trying to soften its image, but it's smoke and mirrors."

The policy is more than two years in the making. It grows out of a commitment Mr. Bush made on the campaign trail in 2000 and again in February 2001, in a State of the Union–style address, when he said of racial profiling: "It's wrong, and we will end it in America."

At that time, profiling had become a growing concern to many blacks and Hispanics, who said that they were being disproportionately subjected to traffic stops, searches, and other law enforcement tactics. Civil rights leaders coined a derisive name for the practice—"Driving While Black"—and the Clinton administration intervened in New Jersey to prevent racial profiling by state highway patrols.

Weeks after taking office, Mr. Bush ordered the Justice Department to conduct a review of racial profiling. Officials said the study was delayed by the terrorist attacks of Sept. 11, 2001, even as civil rights groups complained that the government's expanded terrorism investigations had made Middle Eastern men the target of racial profiling more than ever before.

The final report from the Justice Department and the policy recommendations were delivered last week to Mr. Bush, who ordered the restrictions adopted across the federal government, the White House said.

The Justice Department, in a survey of federal operations, concluded in its report that profiling did not appear to be "a systemic problem."

Law enforcement officials cannot use race or ethnicity "as a proxy" to focus increased criminal suspicion on a person.

"The way the president looks at it," a White House spokesman, Scott McClellan, said, "this is about stopping the abuses of a few, and today's action should only strengthen the public's confidence that the vast majority of law enforcement officials have earned and deserve credit for the job they do in protecting Americans."

The Justice Department acknowledged, however, that past policies were often unclear.

Only 7 of the 70 law enforcement agencies surveyed had policies that specifically prohibited racial profiling, and those policies sometimes varied in tone and substance, the Justice Department review found.

Ralph Boyd, an assistant attorney general at the Justice Department who runs the civil rights division, said the over-arching theme of the guidelines is that law enforcement officials cannot use race or ethnicity "as a proxy" to focus increased criminal suspicion on a person.

"This is an antistereotyping guidance" aimed at balancing the civil rights of the public against the legitimate needs of law enforcement, Mr. Boyd said.

The policy lays out two distinct sets of guidelines: a broad prohibition on profiling in traditional and often routine law enforcement investigations; and a looser set of standards for national security cases.

In traditional operations like traffic stops, federal agents "may not use race or ethnicity to any degree, except that officers may rely on race and ethnicity in a specific suspect description," the policy states. Officials said this prohibition was intended to go beyond the safeguards of the Constitution and existing law.

So, for instance, agents conducting drug or auto theft investigations are barred from singling out people or neighborhoods based on the "generalized assumption" that people of a certain race or ethnicity are more likely to be drug dealers or car thieves.

But federal park police who had a description of a fleeing bank robbery suspect—with a specific race and physical description—could use race in deciding which speeding drivers to pull over. The information in such cases must be specific and "trustworthy," the policy says.

In investigations involving national security and border integrity, the new policy adopts a lower standard, saying federal agents "may consider race, ethnicity and other relevant factors to the extent permitted by our laws and the Constitution."

The racial information that the authorities can use in such cases does not have to be very specific. The policy notes that because terrorists have the ability to strike almost anywhere, "there can be no expectation that the information must be specific to a particular locale or even to a particular identified scheme."

Ibrahim Hooper, a spokesman for the Council on American-Islamic Relations, said the new policy would do little to mollify Arab-Americans.

"There seem to be a lot of 'buts' and 'howevers' here that would allow profiling of Arabs and Muslims to continue," Mr. Hooper said.

He said he found the policy paradoxical in light of a report from the Justice Department this month criticizing the detentions of hundreds of illegal immigrants, most of them Middle Eastern, after the 9/11 attacks.

"This is a problem that's certainly widespread, and I don't think this policy does anything to help the situation," Mr. Hooper said.

Ms. Murphy at the A.C.L.U. said she was troubled that the policy was issued as "guidance" from the Justice Department rather than as an executive order from the White House or a legislative proposal. She said the policy might lack teeth—and enforcement mechanisms—as a result.

The Bush administration "is trying to get the public relations benefits of a new law without actually creating a new law," she said.

But the White House said that even without issuing an executive order, the administration was committed to ensuring that the new policy was strictly enforced.

"This guidance comes directly from the president," Mr. McClellan said. "The president directed the attorney general to come up with specific steps to end racial profiling, and this policy comes out of that commitment."

Point: The Case for Profiling

By Sharon R. Reddick
International Social Science Review, 2004

On September 11, 2001 ("9/11"), over 3,000 lives were lost in New York City, Washington, D.C., and Somerset County, Pennsylvania, due, in part, to ineffective airport security. Since that horrific day, air travel has become increasingly unpleasant without necessarily being safer. Profiling, based on both the behavior and appearance of airline passengers, provides a vital tool that effectively and efficiently increases airport security. Before 9/11, racial profiling was a term that most often referred to a "law enforcement practice of taking the race of a potential suspect into account in deciding whether to initiate investigation of that suspect."[1] Before the tragic events of that day, 80 percent of Americans opposed racial profiling.[2] Today, 60 percent of Americans believe in the necessity of some form of profiling to ensure public safety and national security.[3] The threat of terrorism on American soil perpetrated by fanatic Muslim extremists makes profiling necessary for the security of the United States. Clearly, the United States is now engaged in a war against terrorism. Historically, in times of national emergencies, profiling becomes a weapon to combat and monitor America's enemies. Now, more than ever, every weapon available must be utilized to combat terrorists who do not value their own lives or the lives of innocent noncombatants.

Throughout its history, the United States has employed some form of profiling to restrict the activities of its enemies. During World War I, the Sedition Act of 1918—an amendment to the Espionage Act enacted a year earlier to outlaw spying and subversive activities by foreign enemies—required "enemy aliens" to register in each state. Pursuant to the Enemy Alien Act of 1798, an enemy alien (or alien enemy) was defined as a person above the age of 14, born in a country at war with America, then residing in the United States but not a naturalized citizen.[4] During World War II, the U.S. Supreme Court, in *Korematsu v. United States* (1944), affirmed Executive Order 9066 authorizing the creation of military areas from which individuals might be excluded to prevent espionage or sabotage. In the opinion of Associate Justice Hugo Black:

> All legal restrictions, which curtail the civil rights of a single racial group, are immediately suspected. That is not to say that

such restrictions are unconstitutional. . . . To cast this case into outlines of racial prejudice, without reference to the real military dangers which were present, merely confuses the issue.[5]

These restrictions on the civil rights of German-Americans and Japanese-Americans, respectively, were defensive measures based on wartime exigencies, not national origin or race. Today, while the United States is not at war with any particular Arab nation, the majority of terrorists come from Arab countries, are between the ages of 17 and 40, and they are Muslim extremists.

The greatest barrier to profiling is the fear that Americans have of offending anyone. To appease civil liberties groups like the American Civil Liberties Union, airport security officials have foregone profiling in favor of random inspections. This system is impractical, frustrating, and ineffective. Random selection allows a young Arabic-looking man to walk through security while a 90-year-old great-great-grandmother from Arizona is virtually strip-searched. Good manners and respect for everyone will not provide protection against terrorism.

> *The greatest barrier to profiling is the fear that Americans have of offending anyone.*

Evidence suggests that the events of 9/11 could have been avoided had the Federal Bureau of Investigation been allowed to continue its line of scientific profiling that led to the arrest of the so-called "twentieth hijacker," Zacarias Moussaoui, a month before 9/11.[6] The science of profiling was developed from the processes of narrowing a list of suspects by identifying areas of interaction of numerous generalizations belonging to all suspects. Profiling, which relies solely on race, ethnicity, religion, or national origin in selecting which individuals to subject to routine or spontaneous investigatory activities, is inappropriate. Probable cause to target a specific individual is different than profiling based on race. Scientific profiling utilizes mathematical probabilities without relying on race as a major factor in the analysis.[7]

Many agencies and businesses use some form of profiling for a variety of reasons. Airlines which operate in the United States rely on CAPPS II (Computer Assisted Passenger Prescreening, Second Generation), a database system that gathers information gleaned from airline artificial intelligence and other powerful software to analyze passengers' travel reservations, housing information, family ties, credit report information, and other personal data. The CAPPS II system is used to determine whether a passenger is a selectee or non-selectee for heightened security checks. The Federal Aviation Administration insists that, while CAPPS II does not target any group based on race, national origin, or religion, it will be able to greatly reduce the possibility of hijacking.[8] Secretary of

Transportation Norman Y. Mineta describes CAPPS II as "the foundation on which all other far more public security measures really depend."[9]

Thus far, one could argue that profiling based on suspicious behavior, not race, has proven to be a more effective method than technology in combating terrorism. Suspicious behavior formed the basis for detaining Ahmed Ressam, an Al Qaeda operative, on December 14, 1999, at the U.S.–Canadian border. One hundred pounds of explosives found hidden in Ressam's car was destined to blow up Los Angeles International Airport. Ressam's odd itinerary, nervousness, and uncooperative behavior aroused the suspicions of a U.S. Customs agent.[10] The arrest of José Padilla in June 2002 also resulted from profiling. Padilla, an American citizen from Chicago, changed his name to Abdullah Al Amuhajir after joining Al Qaeda. He allegedly participated in a plot to detonate a "dirty bomb."[11] Richard Reid, the "shoe-bomber" who tried to blow up an American Airlines flight from Paris to Miami in December 2001, carried a British passport issued just two weeks before the incident. Reid was traveling alone without any checked luggage.[12]

Since it is possible for an Arabic-looking terrorist to disguise his looks or to recruit someone who does not fit the profile, behavior, combined with ethnicity, offers a better determinant as to whether someone is a threat. Airport security agents should look for signs such as a passenger who is carrying a new passport, has very little luggage, buys a one-way ticket, and pays cash for that ticket. Screening every person entering the airport causes delays. By targeting high-risk persons, airport security officials increase the odds of stopping a potential hijacker.

To be sure, profiling, if abused, can be harmful, but it is necessary. Profiling works in terrorism cases, and it effectively relieves some of the public's fear of terrorist attacks. Profiling, when used correctly, is an effective law-enforcement tool and deterrent against further violence. It provides a means of tracking the whereabouts and activities of suspects and can lead to the capture of terrorist plotters before they have committed their acts of violence.

Endnotes

1. Sherry F. Colb, "The New Face of Racial Profiling: How Terrorism Affects the Debate," *FindLaw*, October 10, 2001, http://writ.news.findlaw.com/colb/20001010.html (accessed June 28, 2004), 1.

2. Nicole Davis, "The Slippery Slope of Racial Profiling," *ColorLines*, December 5, 2001, http://www.arc.org/C_Lines/CLArchive/story2001_12_05.html (accessed June 28, 2004), 1.

3. Robert A. Levy, "Profiling Proposal: A Rational and Moral Framework," *National Review Online*, October 5, 2001, http://www.nationalreview.com/comment/commentlevy100501.shtml (accessed June 28, 2004), 1.

4. 50 U.S.C. §§21-24 (1994). Paul L. Murphy, *World War I and the Origin of Civil Liberties in the United States* (New York: W.W. Norton and Company, Inc.,

1979) provides the best study concerning government restrictions on constitutional rights during World War I.

5. 323 U.S. 214; 65 S.Ct. 193; 89 L. Ed. 194 (1944).

6. Philip Shenon, "Threats and Responses: The 9/11 Defendant; Early Warnings on Moussaoui Are Detailed," *New York Times*, October 18, 2002, A13; Guy Taylor, "FBI finds no evidence of Moussaoui e-mails," *Washington Times*, September 5, 2002, A5.

7. Frederick Schauer, *Profiles, Probabilities, and Stereotypes* (Cambridge, MA: Belknap Press, 2003), 155–74.

8. Robert O'Harrow, Jr., "Air Security Focusing on Flier Screening," *Washington Post*, September 4, 2002, A1.

9. Ibid.

10. Heather Mac Donald, "Will Curbs on Profiling Open a Pandora's Box?" *The* (Bergen County, NJ) *Record*, May 8, 2002, A5.

11. William Smith, "Terrorist Profiling is not Racial Profiling," *USA Today*, June 18, 2002, A14.

12. ABC News, "Al-Qaeda Link: Sources say Shoe Bomb Suspect and '20th Hijacker' had Contact," December 26, 2001, http://abcnews.go.com/sections/us/DailyNews/airplane_explosives011226.html(accessed July 28, 2004), 1–3; ABC News, "No Bail: Shoe Bomb Suspect Stays Behind Bars," December 28, 2001, http://abcnews.go.com/sections/us/DailyNewsairplane_explosives011228html (accessed July 28, 2004), 1–3.

Counterpoint: The Case Against Profiling

BY CHRISTINA FAUCHON
INTERNATIONAL SOCIAL SCIENCE REVIEW, 2004

Racial profiling can be defined as stopping and searching people passing through public areas solely because of their color, race, or ethnicity. Upon close examination of history, current events, the U.S. Constitution, case law, and both the policy itself and its social implications, one finds that racial profiling in any environment, including airports, is an unproductive and immoral policy to ensure safety.

Much like today, the World War II era was filled with fear and uncertainty, leading the U.S. government to incarcerate Japanese-Americans. Within three months of the Japanese attack on Pearl Harbor, President Franklin D. Roosevelt signed Executive Order 9066 which:

> authorized the removal of all persons of Japanese descent from the west coast. Men, women and children of Japanese ancestry were falsely portrayed as a threat to national security and put into concentration camps without trial or individual review even though two thirds of them were U.S. citizens.[1]

In 1980, Congress established the Commission on Wartime Relocation and Internment of Civilians to investigate the internment of Japanese-Americans. The commission determined that a letter of apology and $20,000 payment was owed to the victims of the government's incorrect behavior. The Japanese-American community felt vindicated—their humiliation had finally been officially acknowledged as the government accepted responsibility.[2] The investigation and outcome showed that, in times of war, racial groups are often separated and mistreated out of fear, and that those who have mistreated them live to regret a hasty decision.

Since the 1980s, the practice of profiling has been applied to America's war on drugs. Specifically, law-enforcement officers have detained members of minority groups in vehicles more often than whites. In conducting such stops, these officers assume that minorities commit more drug offenses, which is not the case. "In all of the published studies to date," Northeastern University law professor Deborah Ramirez points out, "minorities are no more likely to be in possession of contraband than whites. Moreover, in many of these studies, minorities, especially Latinos, are less likely to be carrying contraband."[3] Thus, race has not proven to be a valuable or reliable resource in profiling criminals. The well-documented profiling of black people for drug offenses does nothing other than fill jail cells with black dealers and addicts while their white counterparts continue to engage in their illicit business.[4]

Targeting *behavior* rather than appearance has proven to be more successful. As Ramirez reports:

> Customs revamped its stop and search procedures to remove race from the factors considered when stop decisions were made. Instead, Customs agents selected suspects for stops and searches using observational techniques and focusing on specific behaviors. . . . Customs conducted 70 percent fewer searches and their hit rates improved from approximately 5 percent to over 15 percent.[5]

If racial profiling has proven time and again not to be beneficial, it seems logical to stop using a practice that alienates an entire

---

To single out a group of people by race violates equal protection.

---

group of people based on their race, a factor that cannot be changed.

Today Americans are faced with a conflict between the needs of national security and the desire for freedom and personal liberty. We are no longer on a battlefield where the enemy is clearly recognizable. Instead, we live at a time when citizens are frightened by information that everything from apartment buildings and malls to major bridges have become military targets. This constant fear has left Americans looking for some way to identify the enemy clearly. As a consequence, the historically discredited practice of racial profiling has again been instituted in airports.

The principles on which the United States has been built include the accepted wisdoms of freedom. The Fourteenth Amendment of the U.S. Constitution promotes two fundamental ideals to protect against racial profiling: equality and due process. The amendment states, "No state shall make or enforce any law which shall abridge the privileges or immunities of citizens of the United States; nor shall any state deprive any person of life, liberty, or property, without due process of law."[6] To single out a group of people by race violates equal protection: The law cannot protect a group of people that is being singled out for investigation. Furthermore, profiling leaves "[a] feeling of resentment among minorities, [a] sense of hurt, and [an] increasing loss of trust in the police."[7]

While few court cases have dealt with profiling, racial profiling is constitutionally unacceptable. Much of the justification for racial profiling is based on the notion of national security. However, in *New York Times v. United States* (1971), the U.S. Supreme Court ruled that national security cannot be placed above First Amendment rights that guarantee freedom of the press. In writing the majority opinion, Associate Justice Hugo Black declared: "The word 'security' is a broad, vague generality whose contours should not be invoked to abrogate the fundamental law embodied in the First Amendment."[8] Accordingly, national security, because it is not clearly defined, cannot be placed above any of the fundamental rights provided for under the U.S. Constitution. In short, national security is not an acceptable excuse to deny rights by profiling. While the United States government has a duty to protect its citizens from physical harm, it also has a larger duty to protect the ideals upon which the nation was founded and the undeniable rights of its citizenry. Physical harm may come and go over time, but the rights of the people must be protected to the fullest extent at all times if such rights are to remain permanent.

One of the most important factors to consider in arguing against racial profiling is the policy itself and the various societal impacts associated with it. It is impossible to measure the cost of alienating an entire race of people from society, and in no way can protecting the nation be used as an excuse for doing so. No benefits have been derived by targeting one race thus making the cost of such a policy unbearable. In fact, many terrorists have not been Arab, as in the case of the Oklahoma City bomber, Timothy McVeigh, or Richard Reid, the airline passenger who hid explosives in his shoes. While racism may exist in society, it is the duty of the government not to promote it. Yet, profiling in airports does just that! Targeting people returning from Arab countries is one thing, but targeting Arabs in general is quite another. If the doors for profiling are opened, the stage is set for future legislation that could create a police state. It is impossible to know the extent to which profiling can affect the future, but no good result can come from it.

The Western world has often been seen as racist and unfair to minorities. Racial profiling confirms these charges. As Sunera Thobani, an anti-racist scholar, points out:

> While such profiling is being lauded as "a valuable tool of law enforcement," it brings to the fore the historically problematic relationship of color to Western Democracy. Racial profiling reveals, once again, the fundamental character of liberal democracy as a racialized project.[9]

It is the responsibility of democracy and freedom to refute these accusations. Racial profiling is a system that has not worked and cannot work. It impacts more than how people feel; it compromises their rights. More troublesome, it can fuel genocide and other horrendous crimes that civilized, democratic nations deem repugnant and should never tolerate.

Endnotes

1. Donna K. Nagata and Wendy J. Y. Cheng, "Intergenerational Communication of Race-Related Trauma by Japanese-American Former Internees," *American Journal of Orthopsychiatry* 73 (July 2003): 266. For details on the internment of Japanese-Americans during World War II and the push for an apology and reparations, see Peter H. Irons, *Justice at War* (New York: Oxford University Press, 1983); Peter H. Irons, *Justice Delayed: The Record of Japanese-American Internment* (Middleton, CT: Wesleyan University Press, 1989).

2. Michael M. Honda, "Japan's War Crimes: Has Justice Been Served?" *East Asia: An International Quarterly* 18 (Fall 2000): 29.

3. Deborah A. Ramirez, Jennifer Hoopes, and Tara Lai Quinlan, "Defining Racial Profiling in a Post–September 11 World," *The American Criminal Law Review* 40 (Summer 2003): 1195.

4. Samuel R. Gross, "Crime, Politics, and Race," *Harvard Journal of Law and Public Policy* 21 (Winter 1997): 416.

5. Quoted in Ramirez, Hoopes, and Quinlan, "Defining Racial Profiling in a Post–September 11 World," 1195.

6. U.S. Constitution, amend. 14, sec. 1.

7. Randall Kennedy, quoted in Marthias Risse and Richard Zeckauser, "Racial Profiling," *Philosophy and Public Affairs* 32 (Spring 2004): 144.

8. David M. O'Brien, *Constitutional Law and Politics: Civil Rights and Civil Liberties*, 5th ed. (New York: W.W. Norton & Co., 2002), II: 571.

9. Sunera Thobani, "Exception as a Rule: Profile of Exclusion," *Signs* 29 (Winter 2004): 597.

Undermining Antiterrorism

BY DONALD KERWIN
AMERICA, JUNE 23–30, 2003

Over the last two months, thousands of Pakistani immigrants have abandoned their U.S. homes to seek refuge in Canada. Most wait fearfully in shelters and motels in U.S. border cities for their refugee interviews in Canada. The Immigration and Naturalization Service has arrested others who may or may not be released for their interviews. Most of the Pakistanis have lived in the United States for years, and many have U.S. citizen children. They have left behind good jobs and strong ties in their adopted communities. Since December, 650 of them have come to a migrant shelter in Buffalo, N.Y. A typical family—a couple with two U.S. citizen children—arrived on a bleak day in mid-February. The couple had entered the United States on temporary visas in the early 1990s. They built a business that now employs 15 people. They have no ties in Canada, but they fear that their children could not survive deportation to Pakistan.

It should come as no surprise that Pakistanis and other immigrants no longer view the United States as a safe or fair country. Over the last 18 months, targeted communities have seen thousands of their members arrested, detained for weeks without charge, held for immigration violations in a sweeping terrorism probe, called in for interviews, and deported after closed hearings. Late last year, the I.N.S. arrested and detained hundreds of immigrant men from five countries (most from Iran) who voluntarily came forward to register. The detainees had overstayed their temporary visas, although many awaited permanent residency based on approved family-based visas. Earlier this year, the I.N.S. arrested men from another 13 mostly Middle Eastern countries. Pakistanis and Saudi Arabians comprise a third group of registrants. As their deadlines approached, the Pakistanis fled.

The Bush administration has characterized its antiterror strategy as a measured attempt to protect liberty. Civil libertarians argue that it dishonors the U.S. constitutional tradition and amounts to a kind of surrender to terrorism. A greater risk, however, may be that immigrants increasingly view the war on terror as ineffective on its own terms and as a pretext to punish immigration violations. Their loss of confidence in the tactics and goals of the antiterror fight could prove fatal to its success.

The Antiterror Investigation

The government has justified its immigration enforcement measures based on contested theories of national security. According to experts in counterterrorism, the U.S. tactics result from intelligence deficiencies and fear of unidentified Al Qaeda cells in the United States and Canada. Since Sept. 11, 2001, the government's priority has been to disrupt and prevent further attacks.

The Justice Department has likened its investigation to piecing together a "mosaic." Its guiding principle, says Vincent Cannistraro, former head of counterterrorism at the C.I.A., has been to "shake the trees and hope that something will fall out"—a strategy that in the short term "might have value and can disrupt terrorist acts, but whose success is difficult to prove." Intelligence experts have harshly criticized the Justice Department's tactics. As the former F.B.I. director William Webster told *The Washington Post*, pre-emptive arrest and detention "carries a lot of risk with it. You may interrupt something, but you may not bring it down. You may not be able to stop what is going down."

> *The Justice Department has likened its investigation to piecing together a "mosaic."*

"Shaking the tree," moreover, can alienate targeted communities, push sources into hiding, and deny investigators crucial information that they might acquire from monitoring suspects. If the "shaking the tree" approach netted a terrorist, it would be difficult to know this, much less to elicit information from him. "You can scare people," says Cannistraro, "which is actually what's being done, or you can try to win them over and cultivate good relationships with them. Cooperation and long-term relationships are much more successful."

Early in its antiterror investigation, the Justice Department adopted a zero-tolerance approach to immigration violations. In October 2001, Arab-American and Muslim-American leaders met with Attorney General John Ashcroft. The group had learned of immigrants who refused to report death threats and hate crimes because they feared deportation. The leaders asked that a "fire wall" be erected between federal hate crime investigations and immigration enforcement. Mr. Ashcroft rejected this request, however, saying that he would not excuse criminal conduct of any kind. For the participants, this represented a chilling development, signaling that violence against their out-of-status community members would go unreported and that cooperation in the broad antiterror fight could be punished.

Few idealize the presence (or treatment) of the seven million undocumented persons in the United States, but the undocumented do not present a heightened security risk. Nearly 80 percent come from Mexico and Latin America, not nations with a strong Al Qaeda presence. Furthermore, as Cannistraro points out,

Al Qaeda recruits those who do not typically raise immigration "red flags"; its terrorists have overwhelmingly entered the United States in legal status. Thus, antiterror measures that target the undocumented—like sweeps of selected work sites and the use of state and local police to enforce immigration violations—do not effectively enhance security. On the contrary, they reduce the likelihood that the undocumented and their family members, who in many instances are U.S. citizens, will report crimes or assist in the terrorist investigation.

Secrecy

Secrecy has also characterized the antiterrorism investigation. For weeks, families, attorneys, and consulates could not locate persons arrested in the post–Sept. 11 dragnet. Once located, many detainees could not be visited for extended periods. The Justice Department refused to release the names or even the exact number of those held. It categorically closed more than 600 deportation hearings deemed to be of "special interest." It warned federal agencies about disclosing information under the Freedom of Information Act. It authorized the monitoring of attorney-client communications that might be used to further terrorism.

The Justice Department maintains that secrecy is necessary to prevent terrorists from piecing together a mosaic of the investigation. It has even suggested that terrorists will not otherwise know when one of their members has been detained. Harry "Skip" Brandon, former head of counterterrorism for the F.B.I., argues that while certain investigative methods and sources need protection, the government often overstates its need for secrecy, sometimes keeping information from the public that could and should be disclosed. The government's failure to penetrate Al Qaeda and its resulting "woeful human intelligence," says Cannistraro, also casts doubt on the quality of the information that it seeks to keep secret. Secrecy can be counterproductive, since open hearings might prompt others to come forward with relevant information. It also insulates the government's tactics from public scrutiny and criticism.

The Innocent

Only a few of the immigrants arrested in the antiterror probe have been charged with non-immigration crimes or deported on national security grounds. The F.B.I. has exonerated hundreds of others, but the Justice Department continues to label them potential security threats. During a conference in October 2002 that was cohosted by my agency, a Justice official reported that the government had deported some persons with suspected terrorist ties on the grounds of immigration violations, because their removal on national security grounds might have exposed investigative methods. The failure to prosecute suspected terrorists, he said, reflected the difficulty in securing convictions.

The Justice Department has offered a similar rationale for deporting Somali nationals. In response to class-action litigation challenging the Somalis' deportation to a land without a functional government, it claimed that not removing immigrants, "particularly to countries which are believed to harbor terrorists . . . runs the risk of jeopardizing national security." Furthermore, it argued that the removal of the Somalis on other than national security grounds did not mean that they lacked "knowledge of, or connection to, terrorism."

While these claims cannot be verified or disproved, the release of suspected terrorists would contradict everything known about the Justice Department's investigation. "I feel strongly," says Brandon, "that if they had much of any information to go on, they would keep [suspected terrorists in their] custody and control. Once you deport them, you lose control over them." In addition, these statements cast suspicion on the overwhelming majority of detainees who have no terrorist ties. They might also lead to the punishment of innocent deportees in their countries of birth. Ironically, Justice officials refused to release the identities of the post–Sept. 11 detainees, in part because this might stigmatize them as potential terrorists.

The release of suspected terrorists would contradict everything known about the Justice Department's investigation.

Refugees and Asylum Seekers

The national security paradigm does not fit refugees, political asylum-seekers, and others who are fleeing persecution. The refugee process may be the most improbable path that a terrorist could take to try to reach the United States. Yet after the Sept. 11 attacks, the United States halted refugee admissions for two months to review the program's security. By the year's end, only 27,000 of the 70,000 refugees approved for admission had entered the country. Advocates urged that unused refugee slots from 2002 be carried over to 2003, but the president effectively lowered the admissions ceiling to 50,000 this year, reserving another 20,000 slots for use only in the event of regional shortfalls or overriding need. The pace of refugee admission has slowed in recent months—in the first quarter of fiscal year 2003, the United States allowed only 4,023 refugees to enter.

Any security concerns that threaten to eviscerate one of the United States' proudest programs—and one that directly assists the victims of terror—should be quickly resolved. "You need to vet refugees, like anybody else," says Brandon, "but processing small numbers is not a national security issue. It's an issue of government inefficiency or inadequate resources."

Similarly, Haitian boat people, fleeing persecution and poverty, do not present a terrorist threat. In late 2001, the administration began to detain Haitian boat people to deter others from coming. It subsequently announced that it would extend the harsh policies governing the Haitians to other immigrants. All non-Cuban undocumented migrants who have arrived by boat or have been in the country for less than two years will now be subject to expedited return. Even those who have established a "credible fear of persecution" will be detained. The Justice Department maintains that this policy will prevent mass migrations that could divert the Coast Guard from its national security duties. "This is not a national security measure per se," says Brandon, "and may be a misapplication of the national security rubric."

The Sept. 11 attacks also increased the momentum to harmonize U.S., Canadian, and Mexican immigration enforcement policies. Mexican officials estimate that they annually intercept (with U.S. support) 250,000 migrants. It would imperil nobody to interview these migrants and to admit to the United States those who are fleeing danger. Nor does the recent U.S.–Canada safe–third country asylum agreement enhance security. Under it, a migrant who transits through one nation will not be able to seek asylum in the other. When implemented, this agreement will bar 15,000 Canadian asylum claims each year. With limited exceptions, these migrants will not be able to seek asylum in Canada and will be returned to the United States—an outcome that is at best security-neutral.

Reporting Change of Address

The war on terror has also given rise to law enforcement initiatives that, in a perfect world, might advance security but that the I.N.S. cannot accommodate. In July 2002 the Justice Department announced that it planned to enforce rigorously a law requiring immigrants to report changes of address within 10 days. This ignored the I.N.S.'s lamentable history of misplacing documents, including two million in a warehouse in Missouri, and its inability to assume new mandates. Most recently, a federal grand jury indicted two I.N.S. contractual employees in California for allegedly destroying tens of thousands of immigration applications. As the General Accounting Office recently reported, the I.N.S. "lacks adequate procedures and controls to ensure that the alien address information it receives is completely processed."

Since August, the I.N.S. has received 825,000 change-of-address notices, compared to 2,800 in the previous month. It could not process the vast majority of these forms. Moreover, as the G.A.O. noted, immigrants who do not want to be detected will "not likely comply" with this requirement. Since the reporting program operates on an honor system, terrorists could simply provide false information.

Undermining Antiterrorism

Many immigrants understand terrorism intimately; they fled it. It outrages them that their adopted country has become a terrorist target. Immigrants will readily make sacrifices, endure hardships, and support reasonable security measures. They have backed legislation to improve intelligence sharing, to track temporary visitors, to improve monitoring of foreign students, and to tighten visa procedures. They have willingly cooperated with the F.B.I.'s investigation. Yet they increasingly reject the security rationale offered for immigration restrictions. At worst, many of these restrictions undermine the anti-terror fight. At best, they do not go to the heart of the threat. The United States needs to penetrate terrorist groups, improve human intelligence overseas, and develop good sources and relationships with immigrant communities. Vincent Cannistraro puts it starkly: "If you have fingerprinted every Saudi in the United States and one then commits a suicide bombing, these [immigration] measures mean nothing."

Straighten Up and Fly Right

By Heather Mac Donald
The Wall Street Journal, December 2, 2004

One of the highest priorities for whoever succeeds Tom Ridge at Homeland Security should be to take political correctness and a fear of litigation out of national security decisions. From immigration enforcement to intelligence gathering, government officials continue to compromise safety in order to avoid accusations of "racial profiling"—and in order to avoid publicly acknowledging what the 9/11 Commission finally said: that the enemy is "Islamist terrorism." This blind antidiscrimination reflex is all the more worrying since radical Islam continues to seek adherents and plan attacks in the United States.

The government antidiscrimination hammer has hit the airline industry most severely. Department of Transportation lawyers have extracted millions in settlements from four major carriers for alleged discrimination after 9/11, and they have undermined one of the most crucial elements of air safety: a pilot's responsibility for his flight. Since the charges against the airlines were specious but successful, every pilot must worry that his good-faith effort to protect his passengers will trigger federal retaliation.

Transportation's action against American Airlines was typical. In the last four months of 2001, American carried 23 million passengers and asked 10 of them not to board because they raised security concerns that could not be resolved in time for departure. For those 10 interventions (and an 11th in 2002), DOT declared American Airlines a civil-rights pariah, whose discriminatory conduct would "result in irreparable harm to the public" if not stopped.

On its face, the government's charge that American engaged in discriminatory conduct was absurd, given how few passenger removals occurred. But the racism allegation looks all the more unreasonable when put in the context of the government's own actions. Three times between 9/11 and the end of 2001, public officials warned of an imminent terror attack. Transportation officials urged the airlines to be especially vigilant. In such an environment, pilots would have been derelict not to resolve security questions in favor of caution.

Somehow, DOT lawyers failed to include in their complaint one further passenger whom American asked not to board in 2001. On Dec. 22, airline personnel in Paris kept Richard Reid off a flight to Miami. The next day, French authorities insisted that he be cleared to board. During the flight, Reid tried to set off a bomb in his shoe, but a stewardess and passengers foiled him. Had he been kept from flying on both days, he too might have ended up on the government's roster of discrimination victims.

Jehad Alshrafi is typical of those who were included in the suit against American. On Nov. 3, 2001, this Jordanian-American was scheduled to fly out of Boston's Logan Airport (from which two of the hijacked planes—including American Flight 11—departed on 9/11). A federal air marshal told the pilot that Alshrafi's name resembled one on a terror-watch list—and that he had been acting suspiciously, had created a disturbance at the gate, and posed unresolved security issues. The pilot denied him boarding. Alshrafi was later cleared and given first-class passage on another flight.

According to DOT, the only reason American initially denied Alshrafi passage was because of his "race, color, national origin, religion, sex, or ancestry." Never mind that there were at least five other passengers of Arab descent on his original flight, none of

---

Litigation phobia is precisely the mind-set that DOT is hoping to cultivate in flight personnel.

---

whom had been given additional screening or kept from flying. In fact, on virtually every flight on which the government claims that American acted out of racial animus, other passengers of apparent Middle Eastern ancestry flew undisturbed.

If DOT believes that an air marshal's warnings about a passenger's name and suspicious behavior are insufficient grounds for keeping him off a flight, it is hard to imagine circumstances that would justify a security hold in the department's view—short of someone's declaring his intention to blow up a plane. Given the information presented to the pilot, the only conceivable reason to have allowed Alshrafi to board would have been fear of a lawsuit.

And litigation phobia is precisely the mind-set that DOT is hoping to cultivate in flight personnel: 10 days after 9/11, the department started rolling out "guidance" documents on nondiscrimination. While heavy on platitudes about protecting civil rights, they are useless in advising airlines how to avoid the government's wrath. The closest the DOT gets to providing airlines a concrete rule for avoiding litigation is a "but-for" test: "Ask yourself," advise the guidelines, "But for this person's perceived race, ethnic heritage or religious orientation, would I have subjected this individual to additional safety or security scrutiny? If the answer is 'no,' then the action may violate civil rights laws."

But security decisions are never that clear. A safety officer will consider many factors in calculating someone's riskiness; any one of them could be pulled out as a "but-for" element. As American's record makes clear, it is almost never the case that someone gets additional screening based on his apparent ethnic heritage or national origin alone; behavior and no-fly-list matching are key in the assessment. (In fact, about half the complainants in the government's action were not even Middle Eastern. DOT simply assumes, without evidence, that American scrutinized the men because of the mistaken belief that they were Arabs.) A pilot trying to apply the "but-for" test to his own security judgment will inevitably reduce the test to an easier calculus: "Deny passage to someone who is or could claim to look Muslim only under the most extreme circumstances."

In application, the "but-for" test reduces to a "never-ever" rule: Ethnic heritage, religion, or national origin may play no role in evaluating risk. But when the threat at issue is Islamic terrorism, it is reckless to ask officials to disregard the sole ironclad prerequisite for being an Islamic terrorist: Muslim identity or its proxies—national origin or ethnic heritage. (Muslim identity should be at most only one factor in assessing someone's security risk.)

American contested DOT's action, but fighting the government civil-rights complex is futile. In February 2004, the airline, while denying guilt, settled the action for $1.5 million, to be spent on yet more "sensitivity training." American's pilots were outraged. "Pilots felt: 'How dare they second-guess our decision?'" says Denis Breslin, a pilots' union official.

Not satisfied with just one scalp, DOT lawyers brought identical suits against United, Delta, and Continental. Those carriers also settled, pledging more millions for "sensitivity training"—money much better spent on security training than on indoctrinating pilots to distrust their own security judgments. And in the government's wake, the private civil-rights bar, led by the ACLU, has brought its own airline discrimination suits. An action against Northwest is seeking government terror-watch lists, Northwest's boarding procedures, and its cabin-training manual. If these materials got loose, they would be gold to terrorists trying to figure out airline-security procedures.

The first George W. Bush administration tried mightily not to offend the antidiscrimination lobby. It's time to give up that game. From now on, common sense alone should determine security decisions, the only course which can protect all Americans, Muslims and non-Muslim, alike.

III. Detention Without Charge

Editor's Introduction

"**I**t is better that ten guilty persons escape than that one innocent suffer," the English jurist William Blackstone wrote in 1783. Variations on this statement have become commonplace in discussions about due process in the United States, reflecting a widespread belief that suspects should be considered innocent until proven guilty. However, in recent years, as the Bush administration's "war on terror" has escalated, voices calling the prudence of this longstanding belief into question have emerged in the media and elsewhere. While there are many who maintain that the presumption of innocence is a cornerstone of the U.S. judicial system, others fear that allowing terror suspects to walk free is tantamount to giving them license to commit murder. For members of both groups, Blackstone's famous claim that letting criminals escape is better than imprisoning innocent people begs the question: better for whom?

In "False Terrorism Tips to F.B.I. Uproot the Lives of Suspects," from the *New York Times*, Michael Moss reports on a series of post–9/11 incidents in which federal agents, responding to unsubstantiated tips, arrested and detained a number of innocent people. Under sharp criticism from the public, Moss writes, the Bush administration revised its antiterror policies to restrict racial profiling and reduce the likelihood of misguided investigations.

In "On Liberty & Lawyers," originally published in the *National Review*, Andrew C. McCarthy defends the U.S. government's antiterrorism policy, arguing that the exigencies of wartime have always included amplifying security measures in ways that might be considered excessive during times of peace. After a brief discussion of the cases of José Padilla, Ali Saleh Kahlah al-Marri, and Yasar Esam Hamdi, suspected terrorists classifed as "enemy combatants" by President Bush, McCarthy claims that the civil liberties of ordinary U.S. citizens are perfectly safe, and that only those who have engaged in suspicious behavior risk being detained without charge. Furthermore, he argues, it is essential that the federal government retain the power to arrest and hold those suspected of plotting attacks, as enemies of the state during times of war are fundamentally different from ordinary criminals. "We are not trying to convict them," McCarthy writes; "we are trying to defeat them."

Elizabeth Amon, writing for *Harper's Magazine*, presents a counterexample to McCarthy's arguments in "Name Withheld." She discusses the case of a Pakistani national who was detained without charge for five months despite the fact that his immigration papers, which had been pending at the time of his arrest, arrived just a few weeks after he was taken into custody. Contrary to McCarthy's claims that only wrongdoers run the risk of being detained under new security measures, Amon writes, "Perhaps the most frightening aspect of the September 11 arrests was, in the end, how arbitrary they were."

Lastly, in "Arraigning Terror," from *Dissent*, Rogers M. Smith argues that recent enhancements of data-sharing networks among government agencies and expansions of federal power to detain, prosecute, and punish terrorism suspects without due process pose serious threats to civil liberties. Describing the U.S. government's treatment of Padilla and Hamdi as "draconian," Smith writes that if federal agents continue to insist that ordinary criminal-justice procedures are insufficient to combat terrorism, they must ensure that civil liberties are safeguarded under any and all new security policies.

False Terrorism Tips to F.B.I.
Uproot the Lives of Suspects

By Michael Moss
The New York Times, June 19, 2003

One evening in late April, the F.B.I. chief in Indiana, Thomas V. Fuentes, went to a crowded basement in an Evansville mosque to ask for help in the fight against terrorism. Some 100 Muslims listened politely.

Then the wife of a local restaurateur spoke up to tell him what had happened the last time agents came calling, shortly after the Sept. 11 terrorist attacks. On a tip, her husband, Tarek Albasti, and eight other men were rounded up, shackled, paraded in front of a newspaper photographer, and jailed for a week. The tip turned out to be false.

But four of the men were then listed in a national crime registry as having been accused of terrorism, even though they were never charged, as the F.B.I. later conceded. The branding prevented them from flying, renting apartments, and landing jobs.

"People were crying as she describes this," Mr. Fuentes recalled. "And at the end, she says, 'My husband was released, and in 19 months nobody has ever said, I'm sorry about what happened.'"

Mr. Fuentes did more than apologize. Last week, at his behest, a federal judge ordered that the men's names be erased from all federal crime records.

The unusual public move to clear the Evansville men of suspicion comes after several terrorism cases collapsed because they were based on tips that proved wrong.

Federal agents, facing intense pressure to avoid another terrorist attack, have acted on information from tipsters with questionable backgrounds and motives, touching off needless scares and upending the lives of innocent suspects.

After a wave of criticism, Bush administration officials have been revising their policies for handling terrorist suspects. On Tuesday, President Bush issued guidelines restricting racial profiling in investigations to "narrow" circumstances linked to stopping potential attacks.

In a report earlier this month, the Justice Department's inspector general found that in the months after the Sept. 11 attacks, many illegal immigrants with no connection to terrorism were detained under harsh conditions.

Federal officials vowed to take corrective steps, including a more careful assessment of anonymous tips. However, they defended their strategy of running most terrorist tips to the ground, calling it critical to thwarting another attack.

But court records and interviews with officials and witnesses show that even seemingly plausible information from tipsters who eagerly came forward to identify themselves has led to misguided investigations.

In Michigan, Mohamed Alajji, a trucker born in Yemen, was jailed for seven days last December before agents interviewed his accuser, who turned out to be making false claims against him to press a family feud.

In Texas, Esshassah Fouad, a student from Morocco, was detained after his former wife accused him of plotting terrorism. She was sentenced to a year in prison for making a false charge. But Mr. Fouad was hit anyway with immigration charges, despite his pleas that he had missed school, violating his visa, because he was in jail.

Even seemingly plausible information from tipsters who eagerly came forward to identify themselves has led to misguided investigations.

The federal and state authorities in Detroit exhaustively investigated accusations by a tipster, Gussan Abraham Jarrar, against seven United States citizens, who he said had formed a terrorist gang called "Whatever It Takes." All of the accusations proved false, and Mr. Jarrar, who had a long record of previous arrests, eventually pleaded guilty to providing false information.

Attorney General John Ashcroft told a Congressional panel on June 5 that he would continue to detain people for as long as it took to ensure that they had no terrorist ties. "Obviously in an ideal world we would like to be able to have cleared people instantly," Mr. Ashcroft said.

But critics warn that law enforcement officials, facing pressure to act fast in running down tips, can too easily leave innocent people mired in suspicion, and alienate possible future sources of good information.

Sorting fact from fiction has always been a challenge for crime fighters dealing with informers, whether they are investigating bank robberies or drug deals. With most tips shrouded in secrecy, there is too little information available from the government to know whether problems with tipsters have increased in the fight against terrorism.

But after the Sept. 11 attacks came a scramble to find any remaining terrorists, and President Bush put out a nationwide call for eyes and ears to be alert.

With thousands of tips coming in every week, the F.B.I. was hard pressed in those early days merely to take in the information, officials said, especially since Justice Department orders were that no plausible tip was to be ignored.

"At one time, when information came to us, a lot of times based on experience the investigator would say, 'Nah, this is not something we will follow through on,'" said Bill Carter, an F.B.I. spokesman in Washington. But after the Sept. 11 attacks, he said, "The director has stated that no counterterrorism lead will go uncovered."

At an F.B.I academy meeting last year, in which strategies for gathering intelligence were discussed, one participant warned that officials were overlooking the effect that pursuing suspects has had on Muslim and other targeted groups.

"I made myself the skunk at this lawn party by saying I didn't think that rounding up people whose names wouldn't be released, and whose civil rights are violated, would allow law enforcement officials to implement an effective plan," said Clark McCauley, a

---

The hope of avoiding deportation by cooperating with the government has led some people to reach out to the F.B.I.

---

professor of psychology at Bryn Mawr College.

Some early tips fell apart in highly public ways, as when a security guard named Ronald Ferry claimed to have found a ground-to-air radio in a certain room in a hotel across from the World Trade Center. The guest who was occupying that room, Abdallah Higazy, was jailed for nearly a month on suspicion that he had helped guide the hijackers who crashed airplanes into the twin towers. Mr. Ferry's falsehood was uncovered when an airplane pilot, who has not been publicly identified, came forward to claim the radio.

A lawsuit Mr. Higazy has brought against Mr. Ferry and the F.B.I. says the agents who took the tip failed to press Mr. Ferry for a sworn statement, to subject him to a lie detector, or to interview a second guard who helped search the room, said Robert S. Dunn, a lawyer for Mr. Higazy.

"They just took his word and ran with it," said Mr. Dunn. F.B.I. officials in New York declined to comment, citing the pending litigation.

The hope of avoiding deportation by cooperating with the government has led some people to reach out to the F.B.I.

The federal authorities say that Hoda Elsaidy, an Egyptian living in California, told them last summer that her husband was plotting to bomb the federal government's Defense Language Institute in Monterey, and that one terrorist cell member had already been paid $90,000 by overseas conspirators.

An F.B.I. agent, according to court records, said the bureau, in turn, promised to help Mrs. Elsaidy resolve a lapsed resident's visa. But after investigating, the authorities concluded that she had made up the story, and she has been charged with providing false information. She has denied the charge.

Her husband, Hany El Nady, was cleared of the terrorist accusation but was imprisoned for other immigration violations and has agreed to leave the country, along with their four children.

Sometimes only the F.B.I gets hurt. John Habenstein, a New Jersey man who presented himself as an expert on Middle Eastern affairs, sent agents scurrying on a sweeping and time-consuming search of a ship for weapons of mass destruction. He later admitted that he had lied in order to promote himself as terrorism expert for hire. But when suspects are involved, officials are having a hard time deciding when to close cases and clear names.

In the Evansville case, the F.B.I. defended its decision to detain the nine men and blamed local jailers for the incident in which the men were photographed. The agent in charge, Thomas Van Wormer, said 40 agents investigated them for a week, "and at the end we sat down and said these people shouldn't be held."

As for this week's move to expunge their names from criminal records, he said: "They were innocent. Not fixing this would be wrong."

But in other cases, officials say it has been difficult to clear away all suspicion. The case of Mr. Alajji, the Michigan trucker, illustrates the limbo into which terrorist suspects can be thrust.

When investigators got a tip last December that he was plotting a bomb attack, F.B.I. agents tracked him down, searched his rig, and interviewed friends and associates. The United States attorney in Detroit had him charged with Social Security fraud, using the tip and other information from the agents to argue that he should be held without bail.

But one thing investigators had not done was talk to the tipster, who named Mr. Alajji using a hot line for terrorist tips. When agents did so nine days later—pressed by a skeptical judge—the bombing plot went up in smoke. "He recanted," said Eric M. Straus, the assistant United States attorney who handled the case.

Mr. Alajji had divorced the tipster's sister, and she was fighting to regain custody of their children, according to people on both sides of the family feud. Prosecutors decided not to press charges against the tipster.

Matters only got worse for the federal team when the judge threw out the fraud charge as unsubstantiated, dismissing the prosecutor with a stinging reference to George Orwell's work on "totalitarian government."

Mr. Alajji was set free, but says the ordeal wrecked his business and compelled him to return to Yemen.

"I did not feel safe in the U.S.," Mr. Alajji said in a telephone interview. "I felt I was being watched all the time, and the prosecutors decided that the file would remain open and I could be arrested at any time."

Mr. Straus says there was other information beyond the false bombing tip that cast suspicion on Mr. Alajji. As for the swift jailing, Mr. Straus said he and other prosecutors simply had no choice, given the magnitude of the threat. "With terrorism you do not have the luxury of sometimes waiting to figure out if the guy is truly a terrorist."

On Liberty & Lawyers

By Andrew C. McCarthy
National Review, April 30, 2004

In a very real way, listening to the Supreme Court of the United States spend two days poring over the implications of detaining enemy combatants during wartime should fill any American with a deep sense of pride. One is reminded how singular a privilege it is to live in a nation that so venerates liberty it will bestir itself to agitate even over the liberty of those trying to annihilate us—not so much because of what it means to them as what it says about us.

It is, though, a tempered pride. "Liberty" so readily evanesces from a concrete circumstance to a lofty universal aspiration to a propagandist's jingo. As it makes that warped transition, it increasingly resides in a vacuum, ever more remote from the real world, where it must compete with other facts on the ground. Facts like this one: It's no longer September 10, 2001. That old world is gone forever.

The dismaying part about the arguments in the three combatants' cases the Court is grappling with—one heard last week concerning foreign combatants detained in Guantanamo Bay and two on Wednesday dealing with American citizens held in military brigs here at home—is that it's principally Liberty the Jingo that is at issue. We are breathlessly warned that the Constitution is under assault; George W. Bush has torn it asunder by declaring the right to lock up anyone—meaning any American, in any place, at any time—and hold him indefinitely, or until the end of the vaporous "War on Terror," which could take, as Justice O'Connor speculated, 25 to 50 years. At Guantanamo Bay, moreover, the President is claimed to have erected a lawless black hole, away from the watchful eyes and jurisdiction of federal judges, for encaging foreigners on the mere suspicion of being Muslim. Liberty, the scaremongers wail, is besieged.

How far is the propaganda from the reality? Well, the war is now over 30 months old. During that time, in a nation of about 300 million American citizens, the president has designated exactly three—three—American citizens as enemy combatants. One, José Padilla (a.k.a. "Abdullah al Muhajir"), who trained with Al Qaeda in Afghanistan and urged a post–9/11 mission involving the detonation of a radioactive "dirty bomb" in a major American city, is said to have been dispatched here by Al Qaeda's operational leaders to conduct massive attacks on dense residential areas and industrial infrastructure. Another, Ali Saleh Kahlah al-Marri, is alleged to have been part of a sleeper cell activated post–9/11 in the U.S. for a second wave of attacks (the government has tied him by phone records to a suspected 9/11 financier, whose number, in the run-up to the suicide hijackings, was also called by ringleader Mohammed Atta). The third, Yasar Esam Hamdi, was captured while armed on the battlefield fighting on behalf of enemy forces that even today—as Army Ranger Pat

> *The shock troops of the civil liberties jihad want you to think George Bush is coming for you, too.*

Tillman's combat death in Afghanistan just last week poignantly reminds us—continue hunting and killing Americans.

It is in light of these cases that the shock troops of the civil liberties jihad want you to think George Bush is coming for you, too.

But the caterwauling about the purported liberty interests of terrorists has nothing to do with the reality of liberty for you. Unless there's a colorable case that you are on the verge of indiscriminate mass homicide or are about to tote your AK-47 through Kandahar any time soon, your liberty is safe—and your security to enjoy it is better assured because the people who want to kill you are in the brig.

And what of Guantanamo Bay? These are enemy fighters captured on the battlefield. There is, it bears repeating, a war going on. We could have killed them. Instead, we took the lesser measure of capturing them. As the Defense Department has recently announced, over 10,000 people—enemy forces and their sympathizers—have been removed from theaters of combat in Afghanistan. They were not all shunted off to Gitmo. They were, instead, initially screened to determine whether they were actually enemy combatants, whether they posed a continuing threat to our forces, and whether interrogating them extensively would likely yield intelligence that could help defeat the enemy, save lives, and end hostilities more promptly. Of the roughly 10,000, less than 8 percent, or a little under 800, were shipped to Gitmo, where they have been humanely held and interrogated.

Contrary to the bombast, the military does not have a great incentive to hold captives endlessly. Once their intelligence value is exhausted, detaining them is burdensome, and makes sense only insofar as they pose a mortal threat. As a result, of the original 800 Gitmo detainees, scores have already been released—to the point where we are now holding perhaps 650 prisoners, the ones believed to be most dangerous. And, as *Newsweek* reports this week, releasing many of these may have been a profound mistake—and one made with an eye toward appeasing critics who, we should know by now, will never be mollified as long as even one terrorist's exertions are being impeded. The released detainees are, predictably, rejoining the battle, taking up arms once again against America.

At too many times during the arguments, in the remove and grandeur of a courtroom far, far from the smolder of the battlefield, Liberty the Jingo seemed awfully weighty as it jousted with these and other new world facts. Our nation has been viciously attacked. Three thousand of our fellow citizens were slaughtered. The enemy demolished a staunch symbol of the economy that is the backbone of our free society, while simultaneously striking at the seat of our military might. We are in a state of war, and it is anything but technical. Nearly 150,000 of our armed forces are in harm's way, lining hot battlefields in Afghanistan and Iraq. They are still being shot at, wounded, and killed. Further, the enemy brayed to the world only days ago that it was working, ever working, to plot attacks during 2004 that promise to dwarf those of 9/11—even as the carnage of the last three years still stuns Madrid, Baghdad, Riyadh, Istanbul, Bali, Casablanca, Djerba, and other victims of militant Islam.

> *The idea here is to defeat the enemy, not send it reinforcements.*

Despite all that, it was not the combatants' counsel but the government that was pressed hardest by the Supreme Court, some of whose members were viscerally disturbed about the seeming "indefinite[ness]" of the detentions. No one quibbled with the President's undoubted power to round up combatants in the first hours or days after the 9/11 attacks, but, for goodness sake, it's been two-and-a-half years now, and how are we to know how long these people will be held without trial?

It's the kind of abstraction closest to a lawyer's heart: the argument based on some hypothetical abuse peculiarly detached from the facts on the ground. Thirty months would indeed be a long time if the last shots had been fired long ago. As it happens, there is a very live war going on. It is a war that will destroy all of our liberties if we don't win. But part of the Court plainly wants the government to pick a number out of the air—30 months? three years? five? Some arbitrary time, unrelated to the progress of the war, when it would somehow feel like justice to say: You've held them long enough—charge them with crimes or let them go.

This misses two core points. First, as already noted, letting them go while hostilities rage means letting them go shoot at our troops or terrorize our homeland. The idea here is to defeat the enemy, not send it reinforcements. Second, the arguments seemed devoid of any sense of how harmful court proceedings could be to an ongoing war. Justice Breyer opined that we use the court system all the time to neutralize bad guys—as if Congress had authorized the President after 9/11 to fight the Latin Kings or the Bonanno Family. At least twice, Justice Ginsberg matter-of-factly asserted that the combatants must be presumed innocent. Well, with due respect, no. They are not criminal defendants—at least not now.

They are enemy combatants. Upon being confronted by our troops on the battlefield, they are not presumed innocent; they are attacked, killed, or captured. Capturing them is part of the war effort, not a conversion into a court case. We are not trying to convict them; we are trying to defeat them. And we would decidedly not be advancing the urgent national cause of defeating them if we brought them to court, armed them with all the rights of criminal defendants, and had trial judges instruct jurors that they should presumptively be walked out the courthouse door unless the government has produced compelling quanta of proof—evidence the publication of which, through our very public criminal process and generous discovery rules, would arm the enemy, in the midst of the war, with a trove of intelligence about our information, our sources of it, our methods of obtaining it.

Further lawyering the war process, some members of the Court, Justice Souter in particular, factitiously parsed the sweeping use-of-force authorization Congress extended to the President a week after the 9/11 attacks. The government argues, based on the Civil War–era Prize Cases, that the President is independently vested with power to repel threats against the U.S., and that, when that power is enhanced by a congressional authorization, the executive stands at the apex of his constitutional warrant. In this instance, America was brutally attacked, and Congress reacted within days with a joint resolution exhorting the President to "use all necessary and appropriate force against those nations, organizations, or persons" that either carried out the attacks, harbor those who did, or are planning future attacks. It could not be clearer that Congress did not distinguish between Americans and non-Americans—and it was already well known in 2001 that some Al Qaeda affiliated terrorists were Americans, and that some of its cells operated domestically; we had established that during the terrorism trials of the 1990s.

But Justice Souter—seeming oddly insulated from both Al Qaeda's recent threats and its onslaught of international atrocities—appeared to think the President's own authority to meet and defeat threats on the U.S. had petered out within a few days of 9/11. That left the congressional resolution, about which he and others brainstormed that perhaps it didn't really mean what it says. Does the use of force—which indisputably includes killing— really include the less drastic measure of capturing and holding? And, sure, Congress said all "persons," but did it really mean American citizens and those captured on American soil?

This, a friend of mine has jibed, is why people hate lawyers. And it's hard to argue with that. As Justice Kennedy wisely observed, historically declarations of war are simply not written to contemplate every conceivable contingency. But at times, listening to the justices, one imagined future declarations: monstrosities that would look more like the tax code or the federal sentencing guidelines than timely, clear, unadorned directions to do the things that for centuries have been done by nations to vanquish aggressive belligerents.

This also brings front and center a reason why conservatives so often complain about the Court's imperiousness. Even the justices most manifestly troubled did not seem to doubt that Congress could authorize, and the President execute, the use of even overwhelming deadly force. Nor was there real dispute that the power to do the greater necessarily includes the power to do the lesser—that it is appropriate merely to capture and detain those you are empowered to kill. Nor, really, could it thus be credibly questioned that the authorization, as written here, could easily be construed to permit the detention of all enemy combatants until the end of hostilities. But rather than leave it at that, some of the justices want more—a positive statement that the facts of these specific cases were within the ambit of legislative contemplation, as well as a certain date when, regardless of what impact it might have on national security, we can either begin jury selection or open the jailhouse doors.

Of course, even if Congress gave them all that, there would be another case tomorrow with new facts unexpressed in the revised resolution, and the merry-go-round would start anew. More to the point, the give-us-more methodology bespeaks a lack of faith in the political process and ignores that Congress often speaks by not speaking. Maybe there's no new resolution because there's no popular perception of a problem. If the American people were up in arms about the detention of three American terrorists and 650 foreign enemy troops who belong to forces that have thus far killed over 700 of our military and thousands of our civilians, there would be little reason to fear. There would quickly be a plethora of legislation calling for release, or at least greater scrutiny of the administration's actions. If broad coalitions in Congress thought for a second that the president's actions had breached the confines of the post–9/11 resolution, there would be a new resolution, cabining executive action where it had heretofore been excessive. That this has not happened is eloquent testimony to the measure, reasonableness, and humanity—indeed, the American-ness—with which we have met our foes, even as they pursue their holy war.

It is difficult to predict how the combatant cases will be resolved. Oral argument is not always a good barometer of where judges stand on a dispute; sometimes their questions convey a view, sometimes they are merely meant to provoke and challenge, the better to sharpen the debate. In the Guantanamo case, the Court should stay out of it and let the branch responsible for fighting the war—which has done it thus far to great effect and with dignity—decide whom to kill, whom to capture, and whom to hold, without judicial second-guessing. But even if the Court flexes its muscles by seizing unprecedented review power, it is likely to exercise that power deferentially, approving the military's actions and giving our enemies scant reason for hope—although potentially bogging the war effort down in legal process.

The American enemy combatants are a more worrisome call. It would be nice if the Court reaffirmed its World War II era ruling in *Ex Parte Quirin* that being an American does not inoculate an enemy from unlawful combatant treatment; but even if the Court were to lay groundwork for future, periodic judicial scrutiny to ensure that detention remains warranted, it is hard to believe the justices will look past the continuing Al Qaeda peril and swing open the door to civilian trials, and all the damage they could wreak, in the middle of a war.

All that, however, is almost secondary. What these cases best display is that liberty, as both an ideal and a reality, is alive and well. For all the pernicious atmospherics, our government has been a model of restraint, and these essential detentions do not foreshadow tyrannical abuse.

Name Withheld

By Elizabeth Amon
Harper's Magazine, August 2003

In its investigation of the September 11 attacks, the U.S. government rounded up hundreds of Middle Eastern, South Asian, and Muslim immigrants. The precise number is unknown. In November 2001, the Department of Justice reported that 1,182 people had been arrested, but it has refused to supply a total since then. This June, a report from its Office of the Inspector General (OIG) chronicled the detention of 762 of the arrestees for violating immigration laws—typically, for overstaying visas. Almost all the September 11 detainees were men, and most remained in custody for months. Many were eventually deported, while others, like M., the man who is interviewed in this document, were released but are too anxious about their immigration status to talk openly to the press. The government has refused to give out the names of the detainees, whom it has labeled "special-interest." In fact, there was little more reason to arrest them than to arrest any of the eight million other out-of-status immigrants living on U.S. soil. Neither M. nor any of the other detainees was shown to have had any connection to terrorism.

M. lives in a brick home in a neat, middle-class subdivision. When I visited him this spring, a half-melted snowman, complete with carrot nose and coal eyes, was sinking into his front yard. A soft-spoken, middle-aged man with a slight accent, M. is cautious in conversation, and his anger at what has happened to him is apparent only occasionally in his words and never in his manner. In November 2001, he was at home with his young son and his wife, who suffers from lupus, when an FBI agent and multiple INS agents appeared at the door. A co-worker at the medical clinic where M. worked had called the FBI; M., she contended, wore a surgical mask "more than necessary." The INS brought M. to their headquarters for further questioning. Despite the fact that his immigration papers, which had been pending at the time of his arrest, were approved six weeks later, M. spent the next five months in a New Jersey jail.

Beginning in December 2001, lawyers from the American Civil Liberties Union visited several of the New York–area facilities where the detainees were being held. Despite Attorney General John Ashcroft's assurances to the Senate that "all persons being detained have the right to contact their lawyers and families," the attorneys at first had tremendous difficulty gaining access. In some cases, the prisons claimed that they were unable to "prepare" the men for questioning; in others, they were told that the INS had not given approval for the visit. When the lawyers were able to meet with the detained, they wrote up a brief report on each. The notes from M.'s interview, portions of which the ACLU released and all of which was approved for release by M., are at right [omitted here].

A third of the detainees were, like M., from Pakistan, by far the most common country of origin; the next most common were Egypt, Turkey, Jordan, and Yemen. All the detainees were immigrants, and after September 11, at the attorney general's request, the chief U.S. immigration judge allowed their hearings to be closed to the public and even to family members. At least 611 of the detainees were subjected to secret hearings, a practice that the Supreme Court this May allowed to stand as constitutional. The Department of Justice has argued that releasing even the detainees' names would compromise its terrorism investigations, despite the fact that the names of other terrorism suspects—e.g., Ernest James Ujaama in Seattle, Jeffrey Leon Battle in Portland, Sahim Alwan and Yahya Goba in Buffalo—have been trumpeted in the press by Ashcroft himself.

Of the 762 detainees covered by the OIG report, more than 80 percent were in custody by the end of November 2001. At the time, Ashcroft seemed to consider the numbers good P.R., and whenever speaking of the detainees he would take care to invoke "terrorism" once or, better yet, twice. (A typical statement, from October 2001: "Our anti-terrorism offensive has arrested or detained nearly 1,000 individuals as part of the September 11 terrorism investigation.") To this day Ashcroft, in his public statements, continues to imply a link between the detainees and terrorism. But the director of the Center for National Security Studies, which filed a lawsuit to obtain information about the detainees, says that in court papers, government officials never connect the detainees to terrorism. A General Accounting Office report from January 2003 found that nearly half of the DOJ's "terrorism" convictions had been misclassified as such. In New Jersey, 60 of the 62 terrorism indictments touted by the U.S. Attorney's Office involved foreign students who had hired others to take English proficiency tests on their behalf.

At 3:30 A.M. on the morning after his arrest, M. was taken to the Passaic jail and charged with having overstayed his visa—a civil, not a criminal, offense. On September 17, 2001, the INS changed its long-standing policy on immigrant detention, extending the time period that an immigrant could be held without charges from 24 to 48 hours and adding that, in "extraordinary circumstances," arrestees could be held uncharged for "an additional reasonable period of time." The DOJ's definition of "reasonable" has proved quite spacious. Of the special-interest detainees, 317 are known to have been held for more than 48 hours without charges, 36 for four weeks or more, 13 for more than 40 days, and nine for more than

50. Such arbitrary practices of detention contradict even the USA Patriot Act, which required that detainees be charged within seven days.

In December 2001, M.'s work permit and residency application were approved by the INS, and yet he was not released. The following month, the FBI cleared him of having any connection to terrorism, and yet still he was not released. Many detainees spent months in jail after they had been cleared; some had even received orders of deportation, or had volunteered to leave the country. Others were deported so quickly after September 11 that they weren't able to pursue any legal strategies for remaining. In many cases, men were sent to home countries where they had not lived or even visited for decades. The INS deported one Pakistani man, detained for having missed an immigration hearing more than five years earlier, without informing his American-born wife. The man was deposited, penniless, in Islamabad, even though his family lived in Karachi, more than 1,000 miles away.

Requests by M.'s lawyer to have him released on bond were repeatedly rebuffed, even after he had been cleared by the FBI. Most people detained on minor immigration violations, such as M.'s, have traditionally been released on bond until their court hearings. But, as revealed in the OIG report, the Department of Justice in September 2001 ordered a "no bond" policy for all the special-interest detainees, even in cases in which there was no evidence that bond should be denied. Soon thereafter, a new regulation allowed the immigration service to overrule an immigration judge about whether *any* detainee is released on bond, even if he is not suspected of a crime or of terrorist activity. Thus the government trial attorney, who essentially is the prosecutor in an immigration proceeding, is allowed to take on a crucial judicial role as well.

"My wife laughs at me," says M., "because I don't like my shoelace to touch the ground." The dirtiness of jail was an ordeal for M., who saw rats and roaches in his cell every day. More disturbing, the detainees—few of whom were guilty of anything more than having overstayed a visa—were forced to share cells with violent criminals. At the Metropolitan Detention Center (MDC) in Brooklyn, where many of the other detainees were held, conditions were even more brutal. The men were locked down for 23 hours a day and imprisoned in perpetual light. Ostensibly the lights were for videotaping—to ensure that the prisoners were not abused—but when the OIG tried to examine the tapes for evidence of abuse it found that those more than 30 days old had been destroyed. Prisoners at the MDC were routinely slammed against walls by guards and were allegedly taunted with anti-Arab slurs. The OIG's report notes that supervisors had told the facility's staff that the detainees were "suspected terrorists."

In general, only one detained immigrant in five obtains a lawyer, even though doing so greatly increases the chance of success—in asylum cases, for example, by four times or more. Because immigration proceedings are considered civil actions, the immigrant does not have a right to an appointed attorney. M. was fortunate to have worked with the same attorney for 16 years, and to have been able to contact him during his detention. Many of the detainees had no attorney, and the lists of free attorneys at the jails were invariably outdated or incorrect. At the Brooklyn MDC, not a single number on the list was a working number for an attorney willing to take on cases. Prisoners there were not always offered their allotted call per week, and when guards did offer it they employed a cryptic shorthand, asking, "Are you okay?" A call to an inaccurate number on the jail's list was counted as the weekly call. According to the OIG's report, the director of the federal prison bureau was told she should "not be in a hurry" to allow the detainees their telephone calls.

In late April 2002, M.'s request for parole was finally granted; he was released on a $5,000 bond, and had to get himself home by taking a bus to a train and then walking two miles in the rain. Both M. and his wife say they often are unable to sleep as a result of his

> *Perhaps the most frightening aspect of the September 11 arrests was, in the end, how arbitrary they were.*

experience, but they worry more about the impact on their five-year-old son (who sometimes asks, when M. leaves the house for work, "Is Daddy coming home?"). Moreover, M.'s five months of incarceration left his family $30,000 in debt. Despite these emotional and fiscal scars, M. is fortunate in how his case was resolved. Other of the detainees have not come home at all: an Egyptian man was deported and forced to leave behind his American-citizen wife and two American-born children; a Canadian man, originally from Syria, was deported to Syria—in violation of international law—where he disappeared for weeks. For others, detention was literally a physical trial. Two detainees contracted tuberculosis in the Brooklyn MDC. Another detainee there had a broken hand and was refused treatment.

Perhaps the most frightening aspect of the September 11 arrests was, in the end, how arbitrary they were. As a result, millions of other U.S. Muslims and Arabs—many of whom came here, as have immigrants for four centuries, in search of asylum from repression or hardship overseas—now see themselves as potential targets. Most of the detainees did violate U.S. immigration law, and for many Americans this fact seems to have absolved the government for its harsh and capricious justice. But in undermining the presumption of innocence, as well as the constitutional rights to due process, to counsel, and to a speedy and public trial, the Bush Administration has weakened these protections for all, citizens and aliens alike. In the process, it has tarnished American democracy, even as it hopes to export this democracy to the very nations from which these men arrived.

Arraigning Terror

By Rogers M. Smith
Dissent, Spring 2004

After the September 11 attacks, the United States began a sweeping restructuring of the nation's intelligence-gathering and coercive institutions. The administration had two goals: first, to enhance information sharing and analysis among all U.S. military, intelligence, and law enforcement agencies. That task is necessary, though it poses dangers to civil liberties that the Bush administration has ignored. The second goal is to expand governmental powers to detain, prosecute, and convict persons suspected of terrorism without any meaningful procedural protections or oversight by the courts. This endeavor presents far more massive dangers, and the case for its necessity has not been made.

The Bush administration believes the United States is engaged in a wholly new kind of war in which, according to its National Security Strategy, it "must be prepared to stop rogue states and their terrorist clients before they are able to threaten or use weapons of mass destruction against the United States and our allies and friends." Knowing that this policy of preventive warfare is likely to be answered with violent assaults at home as well as abroad, the administration has begun to reconstitute all basic systems for exercising coercive force: the criminal justice system, conventional military operations, immigration control, and foreign intelligence gathering and special operations. It has also distanced itself from the developing system of international criminal law, notably by refusing assent to the International Criminal Court.

So far, the administration has taken five major steps to enhance the nation's ability to detect and deter terrorist threats by restructuring these coercive systems:

1. the passage of the USA Patriot Act on October 25, 2001;

2. the president's executive order issued November 13, 2001, authorizing detention and military trials for non-citizens suspected of terrorism;

3. the opening on January 11, 2002, of the Guantánamo, Cuba, naval base detention camp, where over 650 persons are still detained—the United States has declared them all to be "unlawful enemy combatants," not prisoners of war, without the individualized determinations of status required by the Third Geneva Convention of 1949;

4. the creation of a new Department of Homeland Security on Nov. 25, 2002, which has absorbed many federal programs, including the Immigration and Naturalization Service and its anti-terrorist "Special Registration Initiative" targeted at Arabic and Muslim immigrants, which led to the questioning of roughly 130,000 male immigrants and alien visitors, the deportation of some 9,000 undocumented individuals, the arrest of over 800 criminal suspects, and the detention of 11 suspected terrorists (though on April 30, 2003, the administration announced that the Initiative was ending, so far only requirements for annual re-registration have been relaxed);

5. the creation by presidential order in May 2003 of the Terrorist Threat Integration Center (TTIC), an interagency body with participants drawn from the Department of Homeland Security, the State Department, the Defense Department, the FBI, the Department of Justice, and various intelligence bodies; it reports to the director of the Central Intelligence Agency.

The efforts to facilitate information sharing are warranted because investigators have now shown that, had there been suffi-

---

Innovations in data sharing inevitably pose new threats to civil liberties.

---

ciently effective systems for data sharing and assessment in place, the September 11 attacks probably would never have happened. U.S. agencies actually had in hand solid information that could have been used to prevent the terrorists from entering the country or staying long enough to complete their plans. A number were on the terrorist "watch lists" of one or more intelligence agencies, but the officials issuing visas did not know this. Some of the terrorists were subsequently guilty of immigration violations, and some were also involved in minor legal infractions, providing grounds for deportation. But because their likely connections to terrorism had not been communicated, they were allowed to remain. If the different pieces of knowledge had been consolidated and analyzed, the plotters might well have been stopped long before they could act.

Still, innovations in data sharing inevitably pose new threats to civil liberties. Collectively these changes dramatically transform the American state, breaking down old barriers between foreign espionage operations and domestic law enforcement; the separation of immigration law enforcement from the criminal justice system; and divisions between national, state, and local police agencies.

Both the USA Patriot Act and the Homeland Security Act undermine the wall between foreign intelligence operations and domestic criminal law enforcement that was maintained throughout the cold war. Sections 203, 507, 508, 711, and 903 of the Patriot Act authorize extensive information sharing among all agencies, whether operating at home or abroad, whether federal, state, or local. Criminal records, educational records, and immigrant histories are all included, and so are the fruits of surveillance methods that would ordinarily be deemed to violate constitutional rights if employed by federal, state, or local criminal law officers in more routine investigations. Section 502 authorizes coordinated action among these heretofore generally distinct agencies. The act authorizing the new Department of Homeland Security goes further yet by not only mandating data sharing, but also placing many intelligence-gathering and immigration law enforcement functions under this single new agency. And despite the fact that immigration law violations are not crimes, immigrant data are now being entered into the National Criminal Information Center (NCIC), even if the data have not been checked to see if they are current and accurate. Instead, on March 24, 2003, the attorney general issued an order exempting the NCIC's Central Record System from national Privacy Act standards that require those records to be "accurate, timely, and reliable." And both the Departments of Homeland Security and Justice are seeking to involve state and local police in

---

The old structures of law enforcement reflected important values that are now at risk.

---

enforcement of immigration laws for the first time, the better to root out foreign terrorists. These information-sharing mandates are being pursued through a bewildering variety of new mechanisms, but the new Terrorist Threat Integration Center is intended to serve as the main integrating institution—though how it will do so remains unclear, and inadequate data sharing remains a major problem.

Many of these changes (and more) are needed, but it is also true that the old structures of law enforcement reflected important values that are now at risk. Because the courts have long held that U.S. governmental agents of all types can take actions overseas in regard to non-citizens, which would be unconstitutional if done to U.S. citizens, and certainly unconstitutional if done within the jurisdiction of the United States, many agencies of the U.S. government are in the habit of coercing witnesses, seizing evidence, and detaining suspects without any real procedural safeguards. When agencies long accustomed to acting without regard to constitutional restrictions abroad are allowed to join more fully in law enforcement efforts at home, there is clearly a danger that constitutional protections may be ignored here as well (especially when the administration is pressing to loosen those protections on a number of fronts). Even if intelligence-gathering agencies merely make data available that could not be legally obtained by a domestic agency, the practical result may be that U.S. law enforcement is freed of constitutional restrictions.

The increased intermingling of immigration and criminal law enforcement raises further worries. Some state and local police are concerned that as they get involved in immigration-law enforcement, they will receive less cooperation from immigrant communities, who will fear that any contact with any government agency might end in their deportation. Those fears are sustained, moreover, by the wealth of legal precedents holding that immigration officials can constitutionally take peremptory actions against non-citizens that other law enforcement officers cannot. If state and local police are simultaneously enforcing criminal laws and the more procedurally lax immigration laws, it becomes easier for them to act as though only the latter standards are binding on them. Thus, when we break down the walls between foreign and domestic enforcement efforts, and between immigration laws and criminal laws, we risk increasing the ways in which domestic criminal policing efforts may infringe constitutional rights, for citizens and non-citizens alike.

Those risks are vastly increased by the government's multi-pronged pursuit of its second goal—its efforts to detain, prosecute, and sometimes execute terrorists without regard for most of the procedural safeguards provided by the Constitution or international law. The president's order authorizing military tribunals, in particular, permits aliens suspected of knowing about or being directly involved in terrorist plots to be arrested without any showing of probable cause to a neutral magistrate and with no opportunity to communicate with an attorney. Suspects can then be detained indefinitely, or tried in closed military trials with the aid of military defense counsel, on the basis of any evidence that military officials deem to have "probative value," even if it is hearsay or illegally obtained. Accused persons can be denied the opportunity to see and hear all the evidence brought against them, convicted on a vote of two-thirds of a panel of military judges, without trial by jury, and sentenced to death without appeal to the civilian courts. The Defense Department has since added some additional procedural protections, such as the requirement that guilt be found "beyond a reasonable doubt," but the basic structure laid out in the president's original executive order still remains in effect. And even if persons are acquitted in such trials, the government can still incarcerate them indefinitely if it continues to believe they are national security risks.

Under section 412 of the Patriot Act and its general "war powers," moreover, the administration has claimed similarly broad powers to detain indefinitely *all* persons, citizens as well as aliens, who are suspected of being involved in terrorism or even of being "material witnesses" in terrorist investigations, without ever filing criminal charges against them or permitting access to an attorney. This is the way prisoners captured in Afghanistan and incarcerated at Guantánamo as "unlawful enemy combatants" are being treated.

Though the United States has justified these stringent measures as within the war powers bestowed by the Constitution, the United States has not formally declared war on terrorists, and it is hard to see how it could do so. Legally recognized wars are declared against rival states, not loose networks of organizations and individuals. As a result, the White House, Defense Department, and the Justice Department have defended their actions by using the heretofore obscure 1942 precedent of *Ex parte Quirin*. There the U.S. Supreme Court upheld secret military trials for Nazi saboteurs captured in Florida and on Long Island during the Second World War.

Though it has become common for both government officials and their critics to refer to this case as validating severe measures aimed at "enemy combatants" or "enemy aliens," those terms are not wholly accurate. *Quirin* does not focus on the powers of the U.S. government in relation to uniformed enemy combatants participating in legal international wars. It is instead the main source of the still ill-defined category of "unlawful" enemy combatants. Chief Justice Harlan Fiske Stone's opinion in *Quirin* stressed that lawful enemy combatants "are subject to capture and detention as prisoners of war by opposing military forces" according to international law. "Unlawful combatants are likewise subject to capture and detention, but in addition they are subject to trial and punishment by military tribunals for acts which render their belligerency unlawful." Such tribunals can, he made clear, be constitutionally conducted without the sorts of procedural safeguards, including Fifth and Sixth Amendment guarantees, ordinarily afforded to criminals, or the international law protections granted to lawful enemy combatants. And though most of the saboteurs tried in *Quirin* were enemy aliens, Stone affirmed that, if the U.S. government deems a person to be an unlawful enemy combatant, it makes no difference whether or not the person is a U.S. citizen. National security requires that such persons, too, be subjected to arrest, detention, and secret military trials if the executive branch deems such measures appropriate.

This precedent makes it entirely plausible for the administration to designate all those now involved in terrorism as "unlawful enemy combatants" or "belligerents." Terrorists clearly act "unlawfully," in violation of international laws of war as well as domestic and international criminal laws. But they are not conventional criminals, either in our eyes or their own—so what else can they be but "unlawful enemy combatants"? And if that is what they are, then *Quirin* also makes it plausible to argue that they can be arrested, detained, and secretly tried by military commissions without normal constitutional procedural protections, just as the

Justice Department has been asserting, whether the suspects are aliens, dual nationals, naturalized citizens, birthright citizens, or anything else.

Yet plausible as those positions are, in the current context they have wide-ranging and worrisome implications. Because *everyone* even suspected of being involved in terrorism is by this definition an "unlawful enemy combatant" or "belligerent," then every investigation of possible terrorist activities can result in indefinite detentions and secret trials on the basis of any evidence that gives even minimal credibility to allegations of such involvement. Now consider what these legal powers mean in light of the new pooling of terrorist-related information among foreign and domestic security agencies; national, state, and local law enforcement bodies; and immigration officials that the United States is undertaking. The results of diverse forms of electronic surveillance, so-called "sneak and peek" searches for which warrants need not be shown in advance, questioning that occurs during indefinite detentions, and the mappings of the social networks of suspects, are all bound to produce data on the activities of citizens with whom foreign nationals or immigrants communicate, as well as on their non-American connections. When international and domestic security agencies; national, state, and local police forces; and immigration officials are all entitled to share such information rapidly, even information that has not been checked for accuracy, *everyone* risks being subjected to coercive measures that would ordinarily be deemed unconstitutional, on the basis of evidence that could not survive customary procedural safeguards.

> *American courts have rarely done well at protecting civil liberties in the face of what they perceived as novel national security threats.*

The application of these draconian measures to American citizens has already begun, most notably in the cases of Yaser Hamdi and José Padilla. Hamdi is a 22-year-old Saudi who was born in the United States and therefore also possesses American citizenship, and who was allegedly fighting on behalf of the Taliban and Al Qaeda when captured on a battlefield in Afghanistan. He claims he was a noncombatant. Hamdi has been held for more than two years without formal charges in military prisons in Virginia and was denied access to lawyers until the Supreme Court agreed to examine his detention. Similarly, for well over a year the courts refused to offer any but the most limited judicial review of the confinement imposed on José Padilla, also known as Abdullah al-Muhajir, an American citizen and long-term resident arrested at O'Hare airport. He was detained incommunicado for some months as a "material witness" to terrorist activities, and though officials then accused Padilla of being an "unlawful enemy combatant" involved in a "dirty bomb" plot, he continues to be incarcerated in a military facility in South Carolina without formal charges. Over Justice Department objections, the Supreme Court has agreed to review his case as well, indicating that not even the Rehnquist Court accepts the Bush administration's claim that these actions can be taken entirely without judicial review. Whether that review will amount to more than a rubber stamp remains to be seen, however. American courts have rarely done well at protecting civil liberties in the face of what they perceived as novel national security threats.

What, then, can be done to provide procedural safeguards against abuse of the heightened information sharing that we must have? The Homeland Security Act did provide for the creation of a departmental officer for civil rights and civil liberties. In September 2003, the first such officer, Daniel F. Sutherland, published a "Strategic Plan," which was, however, little more than a promissory note; it did not specify how information sharing would be accompanied by civil liberties protections.

A variety of public and private agencies are providing more concrete suggestions. The congressionally created "Gilmore Commission," formally known as the "Advisory Panel to Assess Domestic Response Capabilities for Terrorism Involving Weapons of Mass Destruction," recommended in its fifth annual report that the president "establish an independent, bipartisan civil liberties oversight board to provide advice on any change to statutory or regulatory authority . . . that has or may have civil liberties implications (even from unintended consequences)." That seems a good idea, but it is doubtful that it could suffice. The advisory board would have no enforcement powers if its advice were ignored and civil liberties invaded.

The panel also repeated a previous recommendation for "a separate domestic intelligence agency" that would be distinct from the FBI's law enforcement activities "to avoid the impression that the U.S. is establishing a kind of 'secret police.'" The report argued that the "'sanction' authority of law enforcement agencies—the threat of prosecution and incarceration—could prevent people who have important intelligence information from coming forward and speaking freely." This proposal is more promising, because this intelligence agency would have neither arrest powers nor immigrant incarceration or deportation powers. Its separation from those activities might help ensure that persons would not be subjected to coercion on the basis of unverified rumors alone. Still, if its information continued to be pooled without adequate checks for validity, the same dangers would exist.

The Gilmore Commission suggests this new domestic intelligence agency would operate under the requirements of the Federal Intelligence Surveillance Act and the Foreign Intelligence Surveillance Court (FISC) that it creates. That court holds closed sessions and can issue secret warrants for intelligence operations. Both Harvey Rishikof, former FBI legal counsel during the Clinton administration, and Thomas F. Powers, a law professor writing in the *Weekly Standard*, have endorsed the alternative idea of a new specialized "federal security court" or "terrorism court" (possibly incorporating the FISC). It would keep anti-terrorist intelligence operations secret while also trying cases with greater procedural protections for the accused than secret military trials afford. But those protections are so far undefined; and as long as this court acted secretly and provided a virtual blank check for all types of intelligence gathering, as FISC has done, it would not be much help in protecting civil liberties.

In December 2003, the Markle Foundation, chaired by Zoë Baird, issued its own task force report, entitled "Creating a Trusted Information Network for Homeland Security." This report focused on the need to enhance information gathering and sharing capacities while also protecting civil liberties and privacy. It argued that the new Terrorist Threat Integration Center must provide "appropriate institutional mechanisms" to achieve these ends. Though these mechanisms remained vague, the Markle task force did recommend the development of standards restricting the purposes to which data could be put, especially unchecked rumors; defining how long such data could be retained; providing for means of data authentication; and establishing regulations governing access to these data. It urged the president to issue an executive order providing such guidelines. While recognizing that "increased information sharing among law enforcement and intelligence entities is critical to the counterterrorism mission," the report expressed great concern that as 2004 began, "no clear government-wide direction has been established for appropriate handling of domestic information while protecting civil liberties."

So far, the administration has not responded to these suggestions or provided any such direction. It has only repeatedly disparaged one further alternative for protecting civil liberties—an option that has, however, never been truly discredited: the existing judicial system.

Though greater information sharing is surely required, why can't we, once we begin sharing data efficiently, combat terrorism while relying on domestic and international criminal justice systems? True, terrorists are not conventional criminals, but they are criminals nonetheless. The administration insists that it is too dangerous to delay detentions and prosecutions of terrorists until law enforcement agencies can constitutionally obtain sufficient evidence of criminal conspiracy to meet "probable cause" standards for arrest and "reasonable doubt" standards for conviction. The Justice Department also contends that covert intelligence operations would be seriously hindered if accused terrorists could see the evidence and witnesses against them. And Bush officials simply distrust international criminal justice institutions, believing that they will be used for political purposes against the United States.

But again, reports by congressional investigators and private news agencies indicate that the real problems preceding the September 11 attacks were not that we used only the criminal justice system to prosecute terrorists, nor that we did not have sufficient intelligence to identify likely terrorists. The main problems were failure to share and analyze data that we had. We also have ample precedents for conducting at least partly closed criminal trials, with the identities of undercover informants and the details of intelligence operations revealed to judges, but not to the defense attorneys and the accused, when necessary to protect ongoing investigations. Are those procedures too risky at present? There is no clear evidence to that effect, only speculation. And when we are undertaking capital cases, the burden of proof must fall on those arguing for abandoning the constitutional rights that have historically been the most effective, albeit still imperfect, bulwarks of American justice. There is no clear need to suspend those rights—and data sharing itself, with the rights in force, does not increase dangers to civil liberties nearly so much. Nor does the United States have the kind of negative experience with international criminal proceedings that justifies forgoing all efforts to see if they can work.

But if the United States continues to insist that ordinary criminal justice proceedings are inadequate to combat terrorism, and if it continues to restructure myriad institutions to promote information sharing and coordinated coercion, then the government cannot in good conscience ignore the need to make sure that civil liberties are protected in this brave new world of anti-terrorism. If the United States does not establish such safeguards, then many American citizens may increasingly come to feel that they are losing precious freedoms at home, even as Americans and innocent foreign civilians continue to lose their lives in wars that seek to establish freedom abroad.

IV. Regulating Morality: Same-Sex Marriage and Abortion

Editor's Introduction

The articles in the first three sections of this book present civil liberties as a public issue, detailing opinions on the relationship between individual rights, the federal government, and the common good. In this section, readers are invited to consider civil liberties as a more private matter and to evaluate what restrictions, if any, the government should place on such personal events as marriage and childbearing. Recently, same-sex marriage and abortion have emerged as two of the most controversial subjects in U.S. political discourse. While many conservatives believe that both practices should be restricted or banned by law for moral reasons, civil libertarians argue that such values-based legislation would infringe upon the fundamental rights of homosexuals and women. Given their divisive nature, how should these issues be approached by lawmakers? Should they be regulated by the federal government, by the states, or not at all? When and in what ways is it appropriate for governments to pass laws that curtail individual civil liberties on the basis of moral criteria?

The debate over same-sex marriage made national headlines in 2004, when the Massachusetts Supreme Judicial Court ruled that it would be unconstitutional for the state legislature to deny same-sex couples the right to marry. That same year, conservative members of Congress introduced, and President Bush endorsed, a constitutional amendment to ban same-sex marriage in all 50 states. Addressing the controversy in "Sacred Rite or Civil Right?," an article first published in *The Nation*, the Reverend Howard Moody discusses what he calls "the religious and constitutional principle of the separation of church and state." Highlighting the fact that marriage is officially regarded by the U.S. government as a civil union rather than a religious contract, he argues that it is misleading for President Bush and other opponents of same-sex marriage to refer to heterosexual marriage as a "sacred institution." Furthermore, Moody writes, many individuals who fight the legalization of gay marriage base their position on the highly subjective belief "that gay and lesbian people are not worthy of the benefits and spiritual blessings of 'marriage'" and fail to support their views with logical arguments.

In "How Legalizing Gay Marriage Undermines Society's Morals," from the *Christian Science Monitor*, Alan Charles Raul presents a conservative perspective on same-sex unions. According to Raul, one of the main purposes of national law is to ensure that the values and will of the majority are safeguarded; indeed, he notes, "collective moral preferences" have shaped countless pieces of U.S. legislation over the years. Therefore, Raul argues, the Massachusetts Supreme Judicial Court's decision on gay marriage undermined both "the moral fabric of society" and the principle of popular sovereignty.

107

In "Why the Federal Marriage Amendment Will Fail," an article first published in the *Advocate*, Chad Graham offers a historical view of the legal issues surrounding gay marriage. Pointing out that only 17 amendments have been appended to the U.S. Constitution since the Bill of Rights was ratified in 1791, he maintains that a federal amendment prohibiting same-sex marriage would be extremely difficult to pass for the simple reason that "amending the U.S. Constitution is nearly impossible." To support his claim, he cites the expert opinion of David Garrow, a civil rights scholar who asserts that an amendment banning same-sex marriage would be unlikely to pass in Congress.

The latter part of this chapter focuses on legal issues surrounding the subject of abortion rights. In "Abortion Wars: State-by-State Combat," from the *National Journal*, Siobhan Gorman presents a hypothetical scenario in which the Supreme Court reverses its famous 1973 decision on *Roe v. Wade*, transferring the decision of whether and when to allow abortions to the individual states. Outlining what she believes to be the most likely result of such a turn of events, Gorman envisions a "post-*Roe* America" in which abortion issues dominate the public discourse, dividing the nation and prompting advocacy groups on both sides to petition state legislatures for support. While opinions as to the probable fallout of this situation vary widely, Gorman suggests that the outcome would differ from state to state, with some states keeping abortion legal, others banning it altogether, and still others opting for an intermediate position that would allow abortion only under certain circumstances.

Finally, in "Letting Go of *Roe*," from the *Atlantic Monthly*, Benjamin Wittes argues that the Democratic Party's fierce commitment to protecting the *Roe v. Wade* decision has damaged not only the abortion-rights cause, but also liberalism and U.S. democracy in general. According to the author, abortion rights should be treated as a matter of public policy, not constitutional law. While "overturning *Roe* would lead to greater regional variability in the right to abortion," he writes, "this would be a worthwhile choice for pro-choice voters to pay in exchange for greater democratic legitimacy for that right and, therefore, greater acceptance of and permanence for it."

Sacred Rite or Civil Right?

By Howard Moody
THE NATION, JULY 5, 2004

If members of the church that I served for more than three decades were told I would be writing an article in defense of marriage, they wouldn't believe it. My reputation was that when people came to me for counsel about getting married, I tried to talk them out of it. More about that later.

We are now in the midst of a national debate on the nature of marriage, and it promises to be as emotional and polemical as the issues of abortion and homosexuality have been over the past century. What all these debates have in common is that they involved both the laws of the state and the theology of the church. The purpose of this writing is to suggest that the gay-marriage debate is less about the legitimacy of the loving relationship of a same-sex couple than about the relationship of church and state and how they define marriage.

In Western civilization, the faith and beliefs of Christendom played a major role in shaping the laws regarding social relations and moral behavior. Having been nurtured in the Christian faith from childhood and having served a lifetime as an ordained Baptist minister, I feel obligated first to address the religious controversy concerning the nature of marriage. If we look at the history of religious institutions regarding marriage we will find not much unanimity but amazing diversity—it is really a mixed bag. Those who base their position on "tradition" or "what the Bible says" will find anything but clarity. It depends on which "tradition" in what age reading from whose holy scriptures.

In the early tradition of the Jewish people, there were multiple wives and not all of them equal. Remember the story of Abraham's wives, Sara and Hagar. Sara couldn't get pregnant, so Hagar presented Abraham with a son. When Sara got angry with Hagar, she forced Abraham to send Hagar and her son Ishmael into the wilderness. In case Christians feel superior about their "tradition" of marriage, I would remind them that their scriptural basis is not as clear about marriage as we might hope. We have Saint Paul's conflicting and condescending words about the institution: "It's better not to marry." Karl Barth called this passage the Magna Carta of the single person. (Maybe we should have taken Saint Paul's advice more seriously. It might have prevented an earlier generation of parents from harassing, cajoling, and prodding our young until they were married.) In certain religious branches, the church doesn't recognize the licensed legality of marriage but requires that persons meet certain religious qualifications before the marriage is recognized by the church. For members of the Roman Catholic Church, a "legal divorce" and the right to remarry may not be recognized unless the first marriage has been declared null and void by a decree of the church. It is clear that there is no single religious view of marriage and that history has witnessed some monumental changes in the way "husband and wife" are seen in the relationship of marriage.

In my faith-based understanding, if freedom of choice means anything to individuals (male or female), it means they have several options. They can be single and celibate without being thought of as strange or psychologically unbalanced. They can be single and sexually active without being labeled loose or immoral. Women can be single with child without being thought of as unfit or inadequate. If these choices had been real options, the divorce rate may never have reached nearly 50 percent.

The other, equally significant choice for people to make is that of

---

It is clear that there is no single religious view of marriage.

---

lifetime commitment to each other and to seal that desire in the vows of a wedding ceremony. That understanding of marriage came out of my community of faith. In my years of ministry I ran a tight ship in regard to the performance of weddings. It wasn't because I didn't believe in marriage (I've been married for sixty years and have two wonderful offspring) but rather my unease about the way marriage was used to force people to marry so they wouldn't be "living in sin."

The failure of the institution can be seen in divorce statistics. I wanted people to know how challenging the promise of those vows were and not to feel this was something they had to do. My first question in premarital counseling was, "Why do you want to get married and spoil a beautiful friendship?" That question often elicited a thoughtful and emotional answer. Though I was miserly in the number of weddings I performed, I always made exceptions when there were couples who had difficulty finding clergy who would officiate. Their difficulty was because they weren't of the same religion, or they had made marital mistakes, or what they couldn't believe. Most of them were "ecclesiastical outlaws," barred from certain sacraments in the church of their choice.

The church I served had a number of gay and lesbian couples who had been together for many years, but none of them had asked for public weddings or blessings on their relationship. (There was one commitment ceremony for a gay couple at the end of my tenure.) It was as though they didn't need a piece of paper or a ritual to symbolize their lifelong commitment. They knew if they wanted a religious ceremony, their ministers would officiate and our religious community would joyfully witness.

It was my hope that since the institution of marriage had been used to exclude and demean members of the homosexual community, our church, which was open and affirming, would create with gays and lesbians a new kind of ceremony. It would be an occasion that symbolized, between two people of the same gender, a covenant of intimacy of two people to journey together, breaking new ground in human relationships—an alternative to marriage as we have known it.

However, I can understand why homosexuals want "to be married" in the old-fashioned "heterosexual way." After all, most gays and lesbians were born of married parents, raised in a family of siblings; many were nourished in churches and synagogues, taught about a living God before Whom all Her creatures were equally

---

More and more clergy are, silently and publicly, officiating at religious rituals in which gays and lesbians declare their vows before God and a faith community.

---

loved. Why wouldn't they conceive their loving relationships in terms of marriage and family and desire that they be confirmed and understood as such? It follows that if these gays and lesbians see their relationship as faith-based, they would want a religious ceremony that seals their intentions to become lifelong partners, lovers, and friends, that they would want to be "married."

Even though most religious denominations deny this ceremony to homosexual couples, more and more clergy are, silently and publicly, officiating at religious rituals in which gays and lesbians declare their vows before God and a faith community. One Catholic priest who defied his church's ban said: "We can bless a dog, we can bless a boat, but we can't say a prayer over two people who love each other. You don't have to call it marriage, you can call it a deep and abiding friendship, but you can bless it."

We have the right to engage in "religious disobedience" to the regulations of the judicatory that granted us the privilege to officiate at wedding ceremonies, and suffer the consequences. However, when it comes to civil law, it is my contention that the church and its clergy are on much shakier ground in defying the law.

In order to fully understand the conflict that has arisen in this debate over the nature of marriage, it is important to understand the difference between the religious definition of marriage and the state's secular and civil definition. The government's interest is in a legal definition of marriage—a social and voluntary contract between a man and woman in order to protect money, property, and children. Marriage is a civil union without benefit of clergy or religious definition. The state is not interested in why two people are "tying the knot," whether it's to gain money, secure a dynasty, or raise children. It may be hard for those of us who have a religious or romantic view of marriage to realize that loveless marriages are not that rare. Before the Pill, pregnancy was a frequent motive for getting married. The state doesn't care what the commitment of two people is, whether it's for life or as long as both of you love, whether it's sexually monogamous or an open marriage. There is nothing spiritual, mystical, or romantic about the state's license to marry—it's a legal contract.

Thus, George W. Bush is right when he says that "marriage is a sacred institution" when speaking as a Christian, as a member of his Methodist church. But as President of the United States and leader of all Americans, believers and unbelievers, he is wrong. What will surface in this debate as litigation and court decisions multiply is the history of the conflict between the church and the state in defining the nature of marriage. That history will become significant as we move toward a decision on who may be married.

After Christianity became the state religion of the Roman Empire in A.D. 325, the church maintained absolute control over the regulation of marriage for some 1,000 years. Beginning in the 16th century, English kings (especially Henry VIII, who found the inability to get rid of a wife extremely oppressive) and other monarchs in Europe began to wrest control from the church over marital regulations. Ever since, kings, presidents, and rulers of all kinds have seen how important the control of marriage is to the regulation of social order. In this nation, the government has always been in charge of marriage.

That is why it was not a San Francisco mayor licensing same-sex couples that really threatened the President's religious understanding of marriage but rather the Supreme Judicial Court of Massachusetts, declaring marriage between same-sex couples a constitutional right, that demanded a call for constitutional amendment. I didn't understand how important that was until I read an op-ed piece in the *Boston Globe* by Peter Gomes, professor of Christian morals and the minister of Memorial Church at Harvard University, that reminds us of a seminal piece of our history:

> The Dutch made civil marriage the law of the land in 1590, and the first marriage in New England, that of Edward Winslow to the widow Susannah White, was performed on May 12, 1621, in Plymouth by Governor William Bradford, in exercise of his office as magistrate.
>
> There would be no clergyman in Plymouth until the arrival of the Rev. Ralph Smith in 1629, but even then marriage would continue to be a civil affair, as these first Puritans opposed the English custom of clerical marriage as unscriptural. Not until

1692, when Plymouth Colony was merged into that of Massachusetts Bay, were the Clergy authorized by the new province to solemnize marriages. To this day in the Commonwealth the clergy, including those of the archdiocese, solemnize marriage legally as agents of the Commonwealth and by its civil authority. Chapter 207 of the General Laws of Massachusetts tells us who may perform such ceremonies.

Now even though it is the civil authority of the state that defines the rights and responsibilities of marriage and therefore *who* can be married, the state is no more infallible than the church in its judgments. It wasn't until the mid-20th century that the Supreme Court declared antimiscegenation laws unconstitutional. Even after that decision, many mainline churches, where I started my ministry, unofficially discouraged interracial marriages, and many of my colleagues were forbidden to perform such weddings.

The civil law view of marriage has as much historical diversity as the church's own experience because, in part, the church continued to influence the civil law. Although it was the Bible that made "the

---

Even in the religious understanding of President Bush and his followers, allowing same-sex couples the right to marry seems a logical conclusion.

---

husband the head of his wife," it was common law that "turned the married pair legally into one person—the husband," as Nancy Cott documents in her book *Public Vows: A History of Marriage and the Nation* (an indispensable resource for anyone seeking to understand the changing nature of marriage in the nation's history). She suggests that "the legal doctrine of marital unity was called *coverture* . . . [which] meant that the wife could not use legal avenues such as suits or contracts, own assets, or execute legal documents without her husband's collaboration." This view of the wife would not hold water in any court in the land today.

As a matter of fact, even in the religious understanding of President Bush and his followers, allowing same-sex couples the right to marry seems a logical conclusion. If marriage is "the most fundamental institution of civilization" and a major contributor to the social order in our society, why would anyone want to shut out homosexuals from the "glorious attributes" of this "sacred institution"? Obviously, the only reason one can discern is that the opponents believe that gay and lesbian people are not worthy of the benefits and spiritual blessings of "marriage."

At the heart of the controversy raging over same-sex marriage is the religious and constitutional principle of the separation of church and state. All of us can probably agree that there was never a solid wall of separation, riddled as it is with breaches. The evidence of that is seen in the ambiguity of tax-free religious institutions, "in God we trust" printed on our money and "under God" in the Pledge of Allegiance to our country. All of us clergy, who are granted permission by the state to officiate at legal marriage ceremonies, have already compromised the "solid wall" by signing the license issued by the state. I would like to believe that my authority to perform religious ceremonies does not come from the state but derives from the vows of ordination and my commitment to God. I refuse to repeat the words, "by the authority invested in me by the State of New York, I pronounce you husband and wife," but by signing the license, I've become the state's "handmaiden."

It seems fitting therefore that we religious folk should now seek to sharpen the difference between ecclesiastical law and civil law as we beseech the state to clarify who can be married by civil law. Further evidence that the issue of church and state is part of the gay-marriage controversy is that two Unitarian ministers have been arrested for solemnizing unions between same-sex couples when no state licenses were involved. Ecclesiastical law may punish those clergy who disobey marital regulations, but the state has no right to invade church practices and criminalize clergy under civil law. There should have been a noisy outcry from all churches, synagogues, and mosques at the government's outrageous contravention of the sacred principle of the "free exercise of religion."

I come from a long line of Protestants who believe in a "free church in a free state." In the issue before this nation, the civil law is the determinant of the regulation of marriage, regardless of our religious views, and the Supreme Court will finally decide what the principle of equality means in our Constitution in the third century of our life together as a people. It is likely that the Commonwealth of Massachusetts will probably lead the nation on this matter, as the State of New York led to the Supreme Court decision to allow women reproductive freedom.

So what is marriage? It depends on whom you ask, in what era, in what culture. Like all words or institutions, human definitions, whether religious or secular, change with time and history. When our beloved Constitution was written, blacks, Native Americans, and, to some extent, women were quasi–human beings with no rights or privileges, but today they are recognized as persons with full citizenship rights. The definition of marriage has been changing over the centuries in this nation, and it will change yet again as homosexuals are seen as ordinary human beings.

In time, and I believe that time is now, we Americans will see that all the fears foisted on us by religious zealots were not real. Heterosexual marriage will still flourish with its statistical failures. The only difference will be that some homosexual couples will join them and probably account for about the same number of failed relationships. And we will discover that it did not matter whether the couples were joined in a religious ceremony or a secular and civil occasion for the statement of their intentions.

How Legalizing Gay Marriage Undermines Society's Morals

By Alan Charles Raul
The Christian Science Monitor, December 9, 2003

The promotion of gay marriage is not the most devastating aspect of the Massachusetts Supreme Judicial Court's recent decision. The more destructive impact of the decision for society is the court's insidious denial of morality itself as a rational basis for legislation.

This observation is not hyperbole or a mere rhetorical characterization of the *Goodridge vs. Department of Public Health* decision. The Massachusetts justices actually quoted two opinions of the U.S. Supreme Court (the recent anti-anti-sodomy ruling in *Lawrence vs. Texas* and an older anti-antiabortion ruling, *Planned Parenthood vs. Casey*) to support the proposition that the legislature may not "mandate (a) moral code" for society at large. The courts, it would seem, have read a fundamental political choice into the Constitution that is not apparent from the face of the document itself—that is, that individual desires must necessarily trump community interests whenever important issues are at stake.

These judicial pronouncements, therefore, constitute an appalling abnegation of popular sovereignty. In a republican form of government, which the Constitution guarantees for the United States, elected officials are meant to set social policy for the country. They do so by embodying their view of America's moral choices in law. (This is a particularly crucial manner for propagating morality in our republic because the Constitution rightly forbids the establishment of religion, the other major social vehicle for advancing morality across society.) In reality, legislatures discharge their moral mandates all the time, and not just in controversial areas such as abortion, gay rights, pornography, and the like.

Animal rights, protection of endangered species, many zoning laws, and a great deal of environmental protection—especially wilderness conservation—are based on moral imperatives (as well as related aesthetic preferences). Though utilitarian arguments can be offered to salvage these kinds of laws, those arguments in truth amount to mere rationalizations. The fact is that a majority of society wants its elected representatives to preserve, protect, and promote these values independent of traditional cost-benefit, "what have you done for me lately" kind of analysis. Indeed, some of these choices can and do infringe individual liberty considerably: For example, protecting spotted owl habitat over jobs puts a lot of loggers out of work and their families in extremis. Likewise, zoning restrictions can deprive individuals of their ability to use their property and live their lives as they might otherwise prefer. Frequently, the socially constrained individuals will sue the state, claiming that such legal restrictions "take" property or deprive them of "liberty" in violation of the Fifth Amendment, or consti-

We have gone to war on more than one occasion because it was the morally correct thing to do.

tute arbitrary and capricious governmental action. And while such plaintiffs sometimes do—and should—prevail in advancing their individual interests over those of the broader community, no one contends that the government does not have the legitimate power to promote the general welfare as popularly defined (subject, of course, to the specific constitutional rights of individuals and due regard for the protection of discrete and insular minorities bereft of meaningful political influence).

Even the much maligned tax code is a congeries of collective moral preferences. Favoring home ownership over renting has, to be sure, certain utilitarian justifications. But the fact is that we collectively believe that the country benefits from the moral strength growing out of families owning and investing in their own homes. Likewise, the tax deduction for charitable contributions is fundamentally grounded in the social desire to support good deeds. Our society, moreover, puts its money (and lives) where its heart is: We have gone to war on more than one occasion because it was the morally correct thing to do.

So courts that deny morality as a rational basis for legislation are not only undermining the moral fabric of society, they run directly counter to actual legislative practice in innumerable important areas of society. We must recognize that what the Massachusetts court has done is not preserve liberty but merely substitute its own moral code for that of the people. This damage is not merely inflicted on government, trampling as it does the so-called "separation of powers." It does much worse, for when judges erode the power of the people's representatives to set society's moral compass, they likewise undercut the authority of parents, schools, and other community groups to set the standards they would like to see their children and fellow citizens live by. Indeed, it is a frontal assault on community values writ large.

It is thus no wonder that many feel our culture's values are going to hell in a handbasket. Yet, neither the federal nor Massachusetts constitutions truly compel such a pernicious outcome. Indeed, to this day the Massachusetts Constitution precisely recognizes that "instructions in piety, religion and morality promote the happiness and prosperity of a people and the security of a republican government." It cannot be stated better than George Washington did in his first inaugural address: "The foundation of our national policy will be laid in the pure and immutable principles of private morality, and the pre-eminence of free government be exemplified by all the attributes which can win the affections of its citizens and command the respect of the world."

Why the Federal Marriage Amendment Will Fail

By Chad Graham
The Advocate, March 16, 2004

Matt Foreman, executive director of the National Gay and Lesbian Task Force, sighed in relief after President Bush's much-hyped interview on NBC's *Meet the Press* in February. Rumor had it that Bush would tell host Tim Russert that he supports an amendment to the U.S. Constitution banning gay marriage. But the president didn't utter one word on the subject.

"Every day that goes by that he doesn't come out in support of the amendment is a good day for us," says Foreman. Those days may be at an end, however: As *The Advocate* went to press, *The Washington Post* reported that Bush is preparing to endorse a sweeping anti–gay marriage amendment.

Expecting just that constitutional gambit from the far right, gay rights groups are already bracing to fight the mother of all civil rights battles in Congress, which could begin this summer.

Amending the U.S. Constitution is nearly impossible. Only 17 amendments have been added since the original Bill of Rights was ratified by Congress 213 years ago. Even the 1919 prohibition amendment—repealed after 14 years—was a century-long movement in the making. The Federal Marriage Amendment would need the support of every single Republican in the Senate and House of Representatives—in addition to 16 Democrats in the Senate and 62 Democrats in the House. Then it would need ratification by simple majorities in both houses of 38 state legislatures. In some respects Janet Jackson would have a better chance of singing in the 2005 Super Bowl.

David Garrow, a civil rights and Constitution expert who teaches law at Emory University in Atlanta, doubts that such an amendment would make it through both houses of Congress. "Using the federal Constitution to cut back on and limit personal rights and liberties that are recognized by an individual state—that's utterly unprecedented. I think it's very difficult to imagine that you're going to get two thirds of state legislatures to actually do this. There are simply too many public officials out there who not only know enough gay people personally but who are going to be reluctant to put themselves at historical risk."

Yet gay rights groups are not waiting for Capitol Hill lawmakers to learn a history lesson. They see a growing backlash against same-sex marriage across the country. Both Democrats and Republicans supported the 1996 federal Defense of Marriage Act denying federal recognition to same-sex marriages and allowing states to deny such recognition, which was signed into law by Bill Clinton. Most of the candidates for the Democratic presidential nomination don't support gay marriage and have become artful at dodging questions about the issue. And adding fuel to the fire was the February ruling by the Massachusetts supreme judicial court that determined gays and lesbians are entitled to full marriage, not just civil unions.

"I don't think we should underestimate the kind of danger our community is in—in both the Congress and in the states right now," says Patrick Guerriero, executive director of the Log Cabin Republicans, a gay political group. "One thing we don't know is an exact wording of an amendment, whether it be the Federal Marriage Amendment or a watered-down version that is more palatable to

---

Lawmakers who support such an amendment might reap short-term political gain but will do long-term damage to their legacy, [constitutional expert David] Garrow says.

---

folks." If the president were to support the marriage amendment, "he would certainly be jeopardizing the more than 1 million votes from us and our families in the 2000 election," Guerriero says. "Log Cabin would be in a position where it would have to consider whether it would endorse a Republican incumbent."

That's the problem. No one in Washington is sure how the final version of such an amendment would be worded. "I think that storm is brewing within the ranks of the conservative party," says Cheryl Jacques, executive director of the Human Rights Campaign. "There is the Musgrave amendment"—the version the *Post* reported Bush will support—"which strikes not just a definition of marriage but also any benefits that a gay couple might get through civil unions or domestic partnership. There are some who want to make that language more moderate. There are some who want that strengthened."

Lawmakers who support such an amendment might reap short-term political gain but will do long-term damage to their legacy, Garrow says. "Does the national Republican Party want to put itself on the wrong side of history like Southern white Democrats did in the 1950s?" he says. "Will Bush really invest in this? How will this look 40 to 50 years from now? There's no denying that public opinion about gay people has changed over time faster than public opinion on anything else."

Meanwhile, groups from the NGLTF to the Log Cabin Republicans are lining up lawmakers to vote against the amendment, if such a vote is scheduled. With some legislators the groups are making the case that it is a form of gay bashing. "Instead of getting into heavy-duty discussion about gay marriage, we get into conservative principles," Guerriero says about lobbying Republicans. "We talk about the broad nature of the Federal Marriage Amendment. In 10 years a majority of Americans will be on our side on almost every single issue, if they aren't already."

Groups are also banking on the fact that some conservative Republicans don't want the federal government making laws on matters that can be decided by individual states. Even former Georgia congressman Bob Barr, a Republican who championed DOMA, has dismissed the amendment as unnecessary and intrusive.

"Lawmakers who believe the U.S. Constitution is being used as an election-year tool will not support this amendment," says David Noble, executive director of the National Stonewall Democrats. "To say that we will tinker with the U.S. Constitution is extreme, no matter what wording choices they choose."

Abortion Wars: State-by-State Combat

By Siobhan Gorman
National Journal, January 1, 2005

Premise: The Supreme Court reverses its 1973 *Roe v. Wade* decision recognizing a constitutional right to abortion.

Some 1.3 million abortions are now performed each year in the United States. If abortion rights were no longer guaranteed nationwide, the resulting rancor, name-calling, and legal maneuvering would likely exceed even the election-year wrangling we've come to expect in an America torn between "red" and "blue" attitudes.

The abortion fight would become intensely personal for many more millions of Americans: Think race relations, circa 1968. Already, abortion "has become, to a large extent, the civil-rights issue of our time," says Leon Panetta, a former member of Congress who was President Clinton's chief of staff.

Post-*Roe* America would look something like this: The 24/7 news cycle would immediately blanket the airwaves with coverage of the ruling that toppled *Roe*. The morning after the decision, the news would be splayed across the front page of every newspaper in America. Follow-up stories would continue for months. Little else would be discussed on the talk-show circuit, around kitchen tables, or at water coolers.

In five states—Arkansas, Illinois, Kentucky, Louisiana, and Missouri—"trigger" laws designed to ban abortion if *Roe* were overturned could immediately take effect.

Meanwhile, advocacy groups on both sides would rally the troops as the action shifted to state legislatures, which would be newly empowered to ban abortion or restrict it in any way they saw fit. Planned Parenthood and NARAL Pro-Choice America would be suddenly on the defensive and having to build up their grassroots support, some of which would have eroded because abortion rights had been protected for so long. Meanwhile, the National Right to Life Committee and a host of other anti-abortion groups, well organized from decades of trench warfare, would plot their course, state by state.

States that anti-abortion forces targeted as their most-promising prospects would become the new battleground states. "You will see all the force and power [of advocacy groups] come to those states—money, people, information," says NARAL's new president, Nancy

Keenan, explaining what she thinks would happen were *Roe* to fall. "All of the resources will be focused on those states. . . . It's almost hand-to-hand combat."

State legislative and gubernatorial races, especially in states where the governor is the only obstacle to an abortion ban, would attract considerable new interest.

Advocates on both sides of the abortion divide largely agree about this part of a post-*Roe* scenario. Then, they diverge sharply.

Promises

The National Right to Life Committee, which was founded in 1973 in reaction to the *Roe* decision, says its paramount goal is "to restore legal protection to innocent human life." In the view of leading opponents of abortion, repealing *Roe* would be a tremendous step in that direction. Jay Sekulow of the American Center for Law and Justice, envisions a bright future for many children who otherwise would never have been born. But Sekulow expects that few states would enact outright bans. "Various states would

---

Opponents of Roe *predict that its reversal would not lead to the deaths of large numbers of women.*

---

act in differing degrees," he says. "Probably not even a handful of states . . . would outlaw abortion."

Overturning *Roe*, say Sekulow and his allies, would dissuade a great many women from having abortions and would encourage sexually active couples to use contraception. "When abortion on demand is available, a lot of women and young girls are pressured into having abortions without being presented with any options," says Douglas Johnson, legislative director of the National Right to Life Committee. He cites a Mississippi study that found a 15 percent decline in abortions after the state instituted a 24-hour waiting period and required pre-abortion counseling.

Johnson contends that many women now rely on abortion as after-the-fact contraception. He points to a study indicating that teen pregnancy rates declined 19 percent in Minnesota after that state began requiring that parents be notified if a minor sought an abortion.

Noting that relatively few American women died from illegal abortions in the years immediately before *Roe*, opponents of *Roe* predict that its reversal would not lead to the deaths of large numbers of women.

Fears

For abortion-rights advocates like Keenan, a post-*Roe* world looks bleak, with abortion banned in as many as 38 states and the District of Columbia. "We have majorities of anti-choice legislators in a lot of states," she laments. "In the states where the deck is so stacked with anti-choice officials, they can just one day ram [a ban] right through." (The Center for Reproductive Rights estimates that 21 states might outlaw abortion.)

Then there's Keenan's nightmare scenario: "There is also the possibility that Congress would enact legislation to outlaw abortion across all 50 states," she says. "Given the composition of Congress, this causes pause."

Keenan says that her most immediate post-*Roe* worry would be that women in some of the states with trigger laws would be forced to travel out of state, perhaps at great expense, to obtain an abortion, as was the case before *Roe*. With abortions suddenly more difficult to obtain, later-term abortions would likely become more common—increasing the danger to the women's health. And some pregnant "trigger-state" women, especially the poorest and most desperate, would undoubtedly seek to have illegal—and potentially deadly—operations at the hands of back-alley abortionists.

Dr. Kaighn Smith knows firsthand the risks of illegal abortions. He trained at the University of Pennsylvania's hospital and saw his share of abortion deaths. He recalls one incident from around 1960: A woman met someone on a bus who offered to help end her unwanted pregnancy. The woman went to the other rider's home, where a catheter was inserted into her uterus to force a miscarriage. "I spent the entire weekend trying to control this lady's infection. And she died," Smith recalls. "To go back to those days would be a tragedy." He says he was so upset by seeing women die from botched abortions that he began to perform the procedure illegally.

Analysis

A Gallup Poll last year found that while 24 percent of Americans say abortion should be legal under all circumstances and 19 percent say it should never be legal, a majority—56 percent—say it should be legal in some circumstances. The most likely post-*Roe* policy landscape follows a similar pattern, says Emory University law professor David Garrow, author of *Liberty & Sexuality: The Right to Privacy and the Making of* Roe v. Wade. He estimates that 20 percent of states would choose to keep today's status quo, another 20 percent would ban abortion, and the rest would opt for something in between.

Which states would fall into which category is a subject of endless debate. Among those most frequently mentioned as likely to keep the status quo are California, Hawaii, Massachusetts, New York, and Washington. Many of those states liberalized their abortion policies in the years leading up to the *Roe* decision. States most likely to impose total bans are the trigger-law states and the most-conservative Southern states.

The middle 60 percent—the battleground states—would enact a patchwork of laws with varied restrictions on abortion. Among the options, says Garrow: allowing only first-trimester abortions; eliminating provisions that allow minors to get a judge's permission to avoid notifying a parent; and state prohibitions on the use of the "morning-after" pill . . .

"The first question everybody is going to start asking is: Are women going to start to die?" says Kathryn Kolbert of the University of Pennsylvania's Annenberg Public Policy Center. "The answer is, 'Yes, but the numbers will not be as high'" as in the years preceding the *Roe* decision. In 1972, an estimated 39 American women died of illegal abortions, down from about 200 in 1965, 300 in 1950, and 1,700 in 1940. Enforcement of abortion laws would be, as it was before *Roe*, at the discretion of local authorities.

Perhaps the best window into a post-*Roe* nation isn't 1972 America, but America between 1989 and 1992—the time between the *Webster v. Reproductive Health Services* and *Planned Parenthood v. Casey* decisions by the U.S. Supreme Court. The *Webster* ruling upheld a Missouri abortion law that, among other restrictions, requires physicians to test whether a fetus is "viable" before performing an abortion. In dissent, then-Justice Harry Blackmun, the author of the landmark *Roe* decision, proclaimed, "Today, *Roe v. Wade*, and the fundamental constitutional right of women to decide whether to terminate a pregnancy, survive but are not secure."

> *Were* Roe *to be overturned tomorrow,* . . . *"Republicans would suffer tremendously."*
> —Paul Weyrich, Free Congress Foundation

Soon, more states began to test the limits of *Roe*. The Louisiana and Utah legislatures passed all-out bans, which were struck down in federal court. More than 1,000 abortion-restriction bills were introduced in statehouses around the country, according to the Alan Guttmacher Institute, a nonprofit reproductive health research group.

The political fallout from the *Webster* decision is instructive, too. In 1989, months after the decision was handed down, Republicans lost the gubernatorial races in Virginia and New Jersey, largely because of their opposition to abortion rights. "You did have a shift," acknowledges Paul Weyrich, who heads the conservative Free Congress Foundation. "Republicans didn't do well."

Were *Roe* to be overturned tomorrow, Weyrich says, "Republicans would suffer tremendously," because public opinion doesn't support banning abortion. But Weyrich adds that a number of years will elapse before overturning *Roe* becomes even remotely likely. Then, he says, "the question is: Is the public sufficiently inculturated with the idea that, in fact, abortion is the taking of a life and that measures are necessary to protect the unborn?" He says that he and his allies must win the hearts and minds of suburban women. If that happened, he predicts, "the reversal of *Roe v. Wade* could be a success."

Emory's Garrow argues that abortion-rights advocates are swimming against the tide of American culture, because Americans have become increasingly child-focused in recent decades—and, consequently, are less receptive to arguments that emphasize women's rights. Keenan of NARAL concedes that Weyrich and his allies "have been a bit successful in framing the debate." But she says she's armed to do some reframing: The fight is really about "reproductive health," she says. "It will be a battle to the end," Keenan vows.

> *Pennsylvania would immediately become a battleground if* Roe *were overturned.*

After *Webster*, Kolbert's home state of Pennsylvania tested the constitutional waters in 1989 with amendments to its Abortion Control Act. Kolbert was the lead counsel for Planned Parenthood in its suit against Pennsylvania Gov. Robert Casey, a Democrat who opposed abortion rights and had signed the measure into law.

The Pennsylvania statute required a woman to undergo counseling and wait 24 hours before obtaining an abortion. And it mandated that a married woman inform her husband of her intent to abort. The Supreme Court upheld everything except the husband-notification provision but spent much of its ruling reaffirming the existence of the constitutional right to abortion first recognized by *Roe*. States, the high court declared, may not place an "undue burden" on a woman who seeks an abortion before her fetus is viable.

With its long history of being a front line in the abortion wars, Pennsylvania would immediately become a battleground if *Roe* were overturned. The state is heavily Catholic, and its lawmakers generally oppose abortion rights. Democratic Gov. Ed Rendell, however, strongly favors abortion rights. Yet, as one Rendell aide pointed out, "He can't be in forever. So, who knows?"

Current Pennsylvania law includes the 24-hour delay with counseling, along with a number of regulations on such minutiae as the hallway size for hospitals where abortions are performed. In addition, the preamble to the Abortion Control Act says life must be respected to the extent possible. "A ban would pass" in Pennsylvania, predicts Kolbert. "The only question is whether it would pass by a significant enough margin to override a veto."

Smith, who is on the board of Planned Parenthood of Southeastern Pennsylvania, says that if abortions were banned in Pennsylvania in response to *Roe* being overturned, there would be fewer deaths than in the pre-*Roe* days—not because demand would be lower, but because more doctors would be willing to perform safe abortions illegally. Smith, now a professor of obstetrics and gynecology at Jefferson Medical College in Philadelphia, says that if his state banned abortion he'd perform them illegally, if he were still practicing. "I wouldn't care if I went to jail," he says.

Even if fewer women were to die from abortion in a post-*Roe* future than died pre-*Roe*, a significant number would become infertile from unsafe abortions, Smith predicts. He worries that while patients who have their own doctors would probably obtain abortions relatively easily, poor women wouldn't be so fortunate. He predicts that demand for abortions would decline only minimally if the procedure were outlawed, because he has seen, he says, that women make their decision based on their judgment of what is in their best interests, not based on what's legal.

Pennsylvania has the nation's only state-funded program to counsel women with unwanted pregnancies about their options. If abortion were banned or severely restricted, demand for the program's services would rise considerably, says Kevin Bagatta, president of Real Alternatives, which runs the 128 state centers and serves about 18,000 women a year.

"From my perspective, this program is the future," says Bagatta, who says that if *Roe* were overturned, his office would probably be flooded with calls from around the country. Last year, he said, 19 percent of the women who came to the centers wanted abortions, and another 24 percent said they were being pressured to have abortions. After meeting with counselors who promised the women emotional support during and after pregnancy if they chose to give birth, 92 percent of those women elected not to abort, says Bagatta. "It's a program that empowers women," he says, adding, "We don't have to wait for *Roe v. Wade* to be overturned to do this."

The wait could be endless. Emory's Garrow places the odds of *Roe* being overturned at "infinitesimal or downright zero."

Letting Go of *Roe*

By Benjamin Wittes
Atlantic Monthly, January/February 2005

Are we about to suffer through another horrible Supreme Court nomination dominated by abortion politics?

Bet on it. With Chief Justice William Rehnquist seriously ill, the prospect of a Supreme Court vacancy early in George Bush's second term looms over American politics. The script for this—and every—Republican high-court nomination was written long ago. You already know how it goes: Both his own convictions and the need to keep his political base happy require a conservative president to nominate someone expected to vote to overturn *Roe v. Wade*, the 1973 case that established the constitutional right of women to terminate their pregnancies. He has only two realistic choices. He can name someone openly hostile to *Roe*—and thereby trigger a major confrontation with liberal interest groups and Senate Democrats. Or he can name someone with no record on abortion rights but whose jurisprudential approach suggests a predictable skepticism toward them—in which case liberals will insist on trying to divine the nominee's views on the question, which he or she in turn will endeavor to conceal. Unless the president nominates someone the Democrats deem it not in their interests to oppose, the nomination process will become an ugly spectacle in which a single narrow issue pushes to the sidelines discussion of the broad array of other important legal questions the Supreme Court handles. And that process will cast abortion-rights supporters as intolerant of those who disagree with them—or even those they fear may disagree with them.

What's the alternative?

Liberal abortion-rights supporters could chill out.

Do you mean surrender and let Roe *die?*

That's exactly what I mean. It wouldn't necessarily come to that, of course. Republicans have put seven of the nine current justices on the Supreme Court—and they still have only one more anti-abortion vote than they had in 1973, when the decision came down 7 to 2. Where reproductive rights are concerned, the bark of a conservative nominee is frequently worse than his bite—as three justices nominated by Ronald Reagan or George H.W. Bush proved in 1992, when, in *Planned Parenthood v. Casey*, they voted that "the essential holding of *Roe v. Wade* should be retained and once again reaffirmed."

Still, if *Roe* ever does die, I won't attend its funeral. Nor would I lift a finger to prevent a conservative president from nominating justices who might bury it once and for all.

Are you a pro-lifer?

Not at all. I generally favor permissive abortion laws. And despite my lack of enthusiasm for *Roe*, I wouldn't favor overturning the decision as a jurispru-

> ## If Roe *ever does die,* I won't attend its funeral.

dential matter. A generation of women has grown up thinking of reproductive freedom as a constitutional right, and the Court should not casually take away rights that it has determined the Constitution guarantees. Stability in law—particularly constitutional law—is critically important; the Supreme Court would do well to remember that. Still, the liberal commitment to *Roe* has been deeply unhealthy—for American democracy, for liberalism, and even for the cause of abortion rights itself. All would benefit if abortion-rights proponents were forced to make their arguments in the policy arena (rather than during Supreme Court nomination hearings), and if pro-lifers were actually accountable to the electorate for their deeply unpopular policy prescriptions.

That's absurd. How can you say that liberalism and abortion rights would benefit if their supporters gave up on the decision that protects reproductive freedom?

By removing the issue from the policy arena, the Supreme Court has prevented abortion-rights supporters from winning a debate in which public opinion favors them.

Since its inception *Roe* has had a deep legitimacy problem, stemming from its weakness as a legal opinion. Conservatives who fulminate that the Court made up the right to abortion, which appears explicitly nowhere in the Constitution, are being simplistic—but they're not entirely wrong. In the years since the decision an enormous body of academic literature has tried to put the right to an abortion on firmer legal ground. But thousands of pages of scholarship notwithstanding, the right to abortion remains constitutionally shaky; abortion policy is a question that the Constitution—even broadly construed—cannot convincingly be read to resolve.

Consequently, a pro-lifer who complains that she never got her democratic say before abortion was legalized nationwide has a powerful grievance. And there's nothing quite like denying people a say in policy to energize their commitment to a position. This point is not limited to abortion. For instance, the host of gay-marriage ballot initiatives in November came in direct response to the decision by the Massachusetts Supreme Court to treat same-sex unions as a judicial matter rather than a legislative one. And less than a year before the Court handed down *Roe*, it single-handedly reinvigorated a public commitment to capital punishment (which at that point was on the way out) by striking down the death penalty as then practiced; within several years states had rewritten their laws, the Court had backed down, and executions had skyrocketed to levels unseen in decades.

But the Court has not backed down on abortion. Thus the pro-life sense of disenfranchisement has been irremediable—making it all the more potent. One effect of *Roe* was to mobilize a permanent constituency for criminalizing abortion—a constituency that has driven much of the southern realignment toward conservatism. So although *Roe* created the right to choose, that right exists under perpetual threat of obliteration, and depends for its vitality on the composition of the Supreme Court at any given moment.

Meanwhile, *Roe* gives pro-life politicians a free pass. A large majority of voters reject the hard-line anti-abortion stance: in Gallup polling since 1975, for example, about 80 percent of respondents have consistently favored either legal abortion in all circumstances (21 to 34 percent) or legal abortion under some circumstances (48 to 61 percent). Although a plurality of Americans appear to favor abortion rights substantially more limited than what *Roe* guarantees, significantly more voters describe themselves as "pro-choice" than

---

One effect of Roe *was to mobilize a permanent constituency for criminalizing abortion.*

"pro-life." Yet because the Court has removed the abortion question from the legislative realm, conservative politicians are free to cater to pro-lifers by proposing policies that, if ever actually implemented, would render those politicians quite unpopular.

In short, *Roe* puts liberals in the position of defending a lousy opinion that disenfranchised millions of conservatives on an issue about which they care deeply while freeing those conservatives from any obligation to articulate a responsible policy that might command majority support.

But if the Court overturns Roe*, won't we go back to the bad old days of back-alley abortions?*

I doubt it. The day the Court overturns *Roe*, abortion will suddenly become a voting issue for millions of pro-choice voters who care about it but know today that the right is protected not by congressional politics but by the courts. At the same time, thousands of conservative politicians will face a dreadful choice: backtrack from the anti-abortion ground they have staked out and risk infuriating their pro-life base; or deliver on their promise to eliminate the right to abortion, and risk the wrath of a moderate, pro-choice majority. In the short term some states might pass highly restrictive abortion laws, or even outright bans—but the backlash could be devastating for conservatism. Liberals should be salivating at their electoral prospects in a post-*Roe* world. The simple fact is that a majority of Americans want abortion legal at least some of the time, and the majority in a democracy tends to get what it wants on issues about which it cares strongly. In the absence of *Roe* abortion rights would probably be protected by the laws of most states relatively quickly.

Sure, certain state legislatures will impose restrictions that would be impermissible under the Supreme Court's current doctrine; some women might have to travel to another state to get abortions. But the right to abortion would most likely enjoy a measure of security it does not now have. Legislative compromises tend to be durable, since they bring a sense of resolution to divisive issues by balancing competing interests; mustering a working majority to upset them can be far more difficult than rallying discontent against the edicts of unelected judges. In short, overturning *Roe* would lead to greater regional variability in the right to abortion, but this would be a worthwhile price for pro-choice voters to pay in exchange for greater democratic legitimacy for that right and, therefore, greater acceptance of and permanence for it.

Hang on a second. This is a constitutional right at stake. You don't argue that blacks should place their civil rights at the mercy of the majority. Why should women? Isn't fighting for fundamental rights a matter of principle?

Indeed it would be, if the right to abortion—like minority civil and voting rights—were unambiguously protected by the Constitution. But let's be frank: it isn't. The right to abortion remains a highly debatable proposition, both jurisprudentially and morally. The mere fact that liberals have to devote so much political energy to pretending that the right exists beyond democratic debate proves that it doesn't.

Lots of fundamental rights are protected by legal authorities other than the Constitution. For instance, the right not to be fired by a private employer because of one's race or religion is statutory, not constitutional. The right to abortion is in no way degraded by the fact that state laws may prove the best means of guaranteeing it. That simply reflects the absence of a national consensus about whether the right exists and, if so, what its limits should be.

This is an easy argument for a man to make. But could you be so blithe if you were a woman, and abortion rights were more than an abstraction?

I have no idea what losing my Y chromosome would do to my attitude toward this subject. But the costs of defending *Roe* have grown too high, and I'm just not willing to pay them anymore.

Do you seriously think that pro-choice liberals could ever come around to your view?

Self-confident liberals already would have. A liberal fear of democratic dialogue may make sense regarding social issues on which the majority is conservative. But it is a special kind of pathology that would rather demand a loyalty oath to a weak and unstable Court decision than make a case before one's fellow citizens on a proposition that already commands majority support. The insistence on judicial protection from a political fight that liberals have every reason to expect to win advertises pointedly how little they still believe in their ability to persuade.

V. Who Watches the Watchers?

Editor's Introduction

Surveillance technology has become such an integral part of everyday life in the United States that sociologists have coined the phrase "culture of surveillance" to describe its effects. In some cases, as with closed-circuit security cameras, surveillance serves as a precautionary measure that allows the watchers to protect themselves and their property from harm. In other cases, as with computer spyware, surveillance is a more aggressive tactic, supplying information for the watchers to use against the watched. On a national level, recent developments in national security policy, particularly in connection with the USA PATRIOT Act, have raised questions about the nature and intent of the federal government's surveillance of civilians. Given that most terrorists operate undercover, is it in our best interests to allow federal agents to monitor our private lives in the hopes of exposing terrorist plots? Or does a proliferation of government-sponsored surveillance risk robbing us of valuable civil liberties? How and in what ways does a national "culture of surveillance" differ from a police state?

In "Technology and Tomorrow: A Challenge to Liberty," from the *Humanist*, Brian Trent argues that the U.S. government has violated the Fourth Amendment by using advanced technologies to spy on ordinary citizens. Since the terrorist attacks of September 11, 2001, he writes, the government's powers of surveillance have been expanded to an unreasonable extent, and federal agents have violated a wide range of civil liberties in connection with homeland-security measures. According to Trent, the provisions of the PATRIOT Act allow government officials to perform intrusive activities with little to no judicial supervision, from monitoring and intercepting private e-mails to conducting searches without warrants, tapping telephones and computers, and examining library and bookstore records: "The digital age's information highway, coupled with increased surveillance systems, makes all information . . . available for unlimited snooping," he argues.

Barbara Dority echoes Trent's anxiety about recent homeland-security measures in "Your Every Move," also from the *Humanist*. According to Dority, the PATRIOT Act has furnished domestic and international law-enforcement and intelligence agencies with new investigative powers and eliminated the checks and balances on those powers formerly held by the judiciary. After criticizing various aspects of the Bush administration's domestic security policy, Dority expresses particular concern that the government will continue its "brazen attacks . . . on the civil liberties of a supposedly free people," thereby jeopardizing the rights, and perhaps even the lives, of U.S. citizens.

In "1984 in 2003?," from the *National Review*, Ramesh Ponnuru claims that many of the concerns that civil libertarians have raised about the USA PATRIOT Act are either misguided or based on erroneous premises. In opposition to Trent and Dority, he maintains that the war on terror is in no way a war on civil liberties, and that it is only because civil libertarians have failed "to do their homework" that they construe the PATRIOT Act as a threat to privacy.

Finally, in "The Patriot Act Without Tears," from the *National Review*, Andrew C. McCarthy argues that the PATRIOT Act has been weakened over the past few years by left-wing and libertarian agitators. As a result, he writes, it has become "perhaps the most broadly maligned—and misunderstood—piece of meaningful legislation in U.S. history." He then proceeds to explore what he perceives to be some of the more successful aspects of the Act, arguing that "if our nation is serious about national security, the Patriot Act must be made permanent."

Technology and Tomorrow:
A Challenge to Liberty

By Brian Trent
Humanist, November/December 2004

It's tempting to wonder if Thomas Jefferson, writing from France to James Madison in support of a Bill of Rights to the U.S. Constitution, ever imagined the possibility of spy satellites. With the Industrial Revolution still in its infancy he would only have the past as his compass when thinking of the days ahead. In fact, the fledgling democracy he endorsed was itself lifted in part from the ancient Greeks. It's reasonable to assume, then, that when Jefferson later sparred with Alexander Hamilton about their new country's future, neither visionary foresaw cameras the size of pinheads or rifle microphones that could detect the conversation of resident redcoats in a building across the street.

Jefferson would have had little to inspire the thought that one day the kilns of human ingenuity would produce devices that directly threaten individual privacy—and test the viability of our most cherished freedoms.

Over two centuries after it was proposed by the first U.S. Congress, is the Bill of Rights destined for the scrapheap? Will liberty survive the age of spy-cams and Patriot Acts, or was George Orwell's *Nineteen Eighty-Four* just a couple of decades shy of hitting the mark?

According to ancient tradition it was the titan Prometheus who, having stolen fire from the gods and given it to humans, inaugurated technological civilization. That pilfered flame which cooked our earliest meals now burns in our atomic reactors.

It also runs in every electronic circuit we use.

As if in defiance of medieval-era opposition to science and technology, modern American society embraces it. Gadgetry of all kinds—often debuting in the markets of Japan's Akihabara—is devoured by American consumers. In the early months of 2004 more people bought camera phones than camcorders, proving the desire for unified, multi-use, compact technologies. The subway commuter can now be chatting with friends, sending e-mail, surfing the Internet, watching an MPEG video, or recording fellow travelers—all with a single device that fits in the hand.

It wasn't so long ago that this sort of gadgetry was reserved for James Bond's Q-branch, compelling 007 to quip, "Quite ingenious!" Now the toys of Ian Fleming's secret agent are the reality of everyday citizens.

And predictably these toys are making legal ripples. In March 2004 a Los Angeles–area man was indicted for allegedly installing a spying device on a computer to record his employer's every keystroke. The $50 device, called a Key Katcher, attaches like a tiny barnacle between the keyboard and hard drive. It then records several months' worth of keystrokes and can later be "debriefed" by downloading its stolen secrets. Naturally, the Key Katcher appeals to suspicious spouses eager to catch cheating mates and to wary parents who want to monitor their children's electronic stomping grounds. In the Los Angeles case, 46-year-old Larry Lee Ropp claims he was acting as a whistleblower by attempting to prove that his company was conducting illicit business practices. Ropp now faces a penalty of up to five years for "illegally intercepting electronic communications."

> *"Tagged" products can be readily tracked through the distribution gauntlet from factory to store shelf.*

While cases like this are destined for legal gladiatorial games, the question that Jefferson might have asked is: "If this kind of spyware can be purchased for merely five bills with Alex's face on it, what *other* sorts of prying-eye technology are available? And what's coming?"

The answer may disturb you.

The Only Thing to Fear . . .

A long-standing practice of biologists is to tag animals with tracking devices so their locations and behaviors can be monitored. In a few short years this technology will be coming to a human near you.

In recent months U.S. manufacturers announced plans to utilize Radio Frequency Identification tags, or RFIDs, in a staggering array of products. Making use of the same technology that allows cars to sail through EZ Pass tolls, RFIDs will be appearing on clothing, sneakers, razors, books, boots, and just about everything else that a tiny tracking device can be stitched onto or into. Why? The initial incentive is a highly practical one: "tagged" products can be readily tracked through the distribution gauntlet from factory to store shelf. Concealed like many extant anti-theft devices, they will do nothing unless touched by a "reader signal," which makes the RFID "reply" with its own unique signal—an electronic dialogue invisible to the person wearing it.

There are other uses for this remarkable invention. The shoppers of 2010 will be able to pass through store checkout lines without needing to pause for any grumpy cashier demanding a price check. The shopper of 2015 will have even better options: imagine being able to walk into a store and have your clothes "tell" the salespeople your entire purchasing history and preferences. As more and more businesses merge into megacorporations, future consumers will find themselves at the heart of an elaborate web work in which their entire financial histories can be traded wherever they go.

This isn't science fiction. Since 1997 Mobil has been spectacularly successful with its Speedpass program while convenience-store juggernaut Wal-Mart has informed its largest suppliers that products must be equipped with RFID tags by January 2005. Obviously, this has raised the hackles of such groups as the American Civil Liberties Union, the Electronic Frontier Foundation, and the World Privacy Forum. It's one thing to install an anti-theft tag on a Liz Claiborne sweater; such devices are removed before you exit the store. It's quite another when your apparel can theoretically announce your location wherever you go.

Then there are the cameras that will study your every move. In Greek mythology, the hundred-eyed god Argus was the world's greatest watchdog; today Argus has become a reality in the form of thousands of surveillance cameras in such key cities worldwide as London, England; Sydney, Australia; and most recently Washington, D.C. After the terrorism of September 11, 2001, the U.S. capital was quick to embrace the cameras, which now keep watchful eyes trained on federal buildings, mass-transit stations, and shopping areas. According to a statement by D.C. Chief of Police Charles Ramsey, America's capital "must and will expand its use of surveillance cameras, much like London, which uses 150,000 cameras to monitor its population."

The use of technology by police to enforce the law is quite different from using technology to monitor a population.

The use of technology by police to enforce the law is quite different from using technology to monitor a population. Arresting lawbreakers isn't the same as tracking every citizen in a given prefecture. Setting up radar speed traps for lead-footed drivers doesn't mean that surveillance should be used on everyone who drives, walks, shops, and has conversations they think are private.

One of the problems with those who shrug off the threat of omnipresent surveillance is they still think these cameras require a rent-a-cop in a security booth whose attention alternates between the grid of TV screens and Gameboys. The alarming truth is that computer recognition technology is improving at such an exponential rate that soon individuals will be identified, logged, and catalogued automatically—without requiring an army of officers scribbling names on a legal pad. Gait-recognition programs sound like something straight out of Monty Python (and in fact the only way to foil them may well be to adopt a particularly silly walk), but they exist, capable of studying the unique nuances in each person's style of step. Facial-recognition programs also have a startling and ever-increasing accuracy record, measuring the distances between eyes, nose, and mouth to come up with a person's ID—sort of like taking fingerprints from afar.

These technologies aren't perfect. Currently if you want to hide from a face-reader you need only don a pair of sunglasses. But given that computer power effectively doubles every few months, don't expect your Ray-Bans to conceal your identity for long. The chilling reality is that, in a society of a million Orwellian eyes, governments can easily slip behind the curtain and establish a police state unlike anything ever seen in history.

Grave New World

"The right of the people to be secure in their persons, houses, papers, and effects, against unreasonable searches and seizures, shall not be violated," reads the Fourth Amendment.

Unfortunately, today the U.S. government has many times run roughshod over these 24 words. Ever since the terrorist attacks on New York City and the Pentagon three years ago, extended powers of surveillance have been granted to the government—and with great rapidity—such that the Bill of Rights has taken a back seat to homeland security concerns. The numerous provisions of the Patriot

The Fourth Amendment rights of the people are on the chopping block.

Act permit monitoring and interception of e-mail, warrantless searches, increased surveillance, and the ability to conduct phone and Internet taps with little judicial scrutiny. They also allow the government to brazenly investigate a citizen's reading habits by snooping into library and bookstore records. On July 8 an effort to curb this part of the Patriot Act barely failed by a vote of 210–210 in the House of Representatives when the White House threatened a veto. A majority was needed to prevail.

The Fourth Amendment rights of the people are on the chopping block. Another provision of the Patriot Act invests the president with the power to label any American citizen an "enemy combatant," in effect dispensing with the Fourteenth Amendment's declaration that "no State shall make or enforce any law which shall abridge the privileges or immunities of citizens of the United States; nor shall any State deprive any person of life, liberty, or property without due process of law." And this is to say nothing about the use of DNA databanks, which are currently unregulated. When will police officers be permitted to demand DNA samples—perhaps by cotton swabbing the mouths of "suspected deviants" in a way reminiscent of 1997's film *Gattaca?*

Is the omnipresent use of cameras a violation of the Fourth Amendment? Many attractive women feel the eyes of men sweeping over their bodies as they walk. But if such an inspection is done by a computer, much more might be surmised. Her vital statistics, financial records, political leanings, press clippings, and all "known associates" could be tallied and scrutinized for whatever an administration deems "deviant or unpatriotic behavior." Wouldn't this qualify as an unreasonable search?

Naturally, this sort of instamatic dossier is only possible if a centralized database of all American citizens becomes available. But these databases are actually under development.

James Dempsey, deputy director of the Center for Democracy and Technology, addresses this very issue in July 2003 in testimony before the House Judiciary Subcommittee on Commercial and Administrative Law. In his paper, "Defense of Privacy Act and Privacy in the Hands of the Government," he writes: "Agencies are developing new 'data mining' technologies that would seek evidence of possible terrorist preparations by scanning billions of everyday transactions, potentially including a vast array of information about Americans' personal lives." While admitting that modern terrorist threats require expanded powers for homeland security, Dempsey suggests caution instead of the hasty fork over of freedoms that politicians did in the fear addled weeks immediately following September 11, 2001. "Government implementations of this uniquely intrusive technology should not go forward without explicit congressional authorization based on a finding of effectiveness, guidance for implementation, and oversight," Dempsey adds.

Consider the development of a data collection system originally known as Total Information Awareness (TIA) from the Pentagon's Defense Advanced Research Projects Agency (DARPA). The system's name was eventually changed to Terrorist Information Awareness, keeping the acronym and purpose unchanged. All available information on a citizen is entered into a centralized database, allowing an agency to make queries on anything and, at the click of a mouse, be provided with a list of anyone who matches the input criteria. Using TIA, a government agency could find all citizens who traveled to Saudi Arabia in the last two years and then cross-reference this list with all citizens enrolled at flight schools. It could also be used to construct a list of all those who attended peace rallies, bought BMWs, went to the library twice a week, and dated women of Japanese descent. The digital age's information highway, coupled with increased surveillance systems, makes all information—or as DARPA puts it, *total* information—available for unlimited snooping.

And it isn't just big government tentacles making use of today's fluid availability of information. Commercial database entities smelling profit are pitching themselves to law enforcement agencies—a few clicks on a wireless handheld device and an officer can access near limitless vistas of private information. And consider entities like LocatePLUS Holdings Corp., a Beverly, Massachusetts, company that proudly announces it maintains databases on 98 percent of the U.S. adult population. Certainly this can be a boon to police. Who, however, is monitoring how this data well-spring is tapped? What watchdog group keeps a wary eye on the compilers of secret lists—not to mention secret courts?

It's not as if there are no historical precedents for agencies like the Federal Bureau of Investigation conducting surveillance on ordinary civilians who—as in the Vietnam-era—wish merely to exercise their First Amendment rights to free speech, freedom of the press, and peaceable assembly.

That the terrorist threat necessitates an increase in the government's power to protect its citizens is entirely understandable. Unfortunately, bills like the Patriot Act have already been used in cases that have nothing to do with terrorism. Last year the Patriot Act was used against a strip club in Las Vegas, compelling Senator Harry Reid (Democrat, Nevada) to quip, "The law was intended for activities related to terrorism and not to naked women."

What Does This Mean for the Future?

In a not-too-distant year an ordinary American—whom we'll call Eric Blair—gets up each day to go to work. Cameras mounted on every traffic light monitor his route. Computers at his workplace door register his arrival and departure. Each time he visits a store, dines out, or attends a movie, cameras controlled by such programs as TIA watch and record him and every purchase he makes.

Blair isn't even a blip in America's surveillance system so long as he sticks to his expected route—sort of like Jim Carey's creepy predicament in the film *The Truman Show*. But one day Blair deviates from his schedule. He calls in sick to work but cameras show him tooling around the city in his car. Perhaps he goes to the library to check out a "politically questionable publication." Perhaps he drives to a girlfriend's house for some "illicit premarital intimacy." Maybe he just wants to find a private place where he can hike—a behavior that suggests "socially deviant tendencies."

This all sounds absurd but the point is that, when everyone can be tracked, *anything* is possible. The policies and philosophies of a given administration, no matter how seemingly preposterous, can be imposed when the infrastructure for universal surveillance exists. Even puritanical "blue laws" for which few people are arrested today could be enforced, as thermal imaging cameras directed at Blair's girlfriend's house are capable of piercing the walls and registering body temperatures suggestive of "illicit intimacy."

Blair's world may have had its roots in 2001 when a terrorist attack in the United States triggered off new homeland security policies. But the surveillance systems originally designed to "look for terrorist behavior" were expanded to "look for deviant behavior." Blair's world is one loosely based on a kind of feudal system of monitoring whereby towns watch their own citizens, states watch their towns, regions watch their states, and regional stations get their directives from the top of this pyramid.

"Such technology must be used only if effective," writes Dempsey in his address to the House committees. "It must be subject to checks and balances; it must be implemented with a focus on actual suspects, guided by the particularized suspicion principle of the Fourth Amendment; and it must be subject to executive, legislative, and judicial controls. At this time, these checks and balances do not exist."

The Eyes of Echelon

For years conspiracy buffs have reported the existence of a shadowy government entity known as Echelon, supposedly led by the U.S. National Security Agency (NSA) in conjunction with its counterpart agencies in Australia, Canada, New Zealand, and the United Kingdom. Echelon reportedly attempts to capture all global communication to and from the United States. This information is then screened by filtering software, or "sniffers," for words and phrases suggestive of subversive content. Since e-mail passes through a limited number of hubs, they're not difficult to screen as they shuttle through.

The possible existence of Echelon has led a worldwide community of computer users to celebrate "Jam Echelon Day." Every October 21 for the past six years people have attempted to jam Echelon's alleged spying eyes by sending out a mass flood of messages containing "red flag" words. And although there are conspiracy buffs convinced that aliens in black helicopters are making crop circles, Echelon really isn't that farfetched; the technology *is* available today. In fact, some of the very hackers who criticize NSA surveillance have themselves hacked into national hubs and installed their own sniffer programs. Once all this information is compiled in one database, Big Brother could be anyone from a federal agency to the teenager next door. Identity theft will explode into a thriving black market industry.

"A despot always has his good moments," wrote Voltaire in addressing the issue of tyranny. "But an assembly of despots? Never. If a tyrant does me an injustice, I can disarm him through his mistress, his confessor, or his page . . . but a company of tyrants is inaccessible to all seductions." In a world of invisible and warrantless searches, omnipresent cameras, and tracking devices, American life may well be thrust under the microscope of a legion of would-be tyrants as inaccessible to "seductions" as they are to public accountability.

Despots throughout history have sought overriding control of their flock and have often achieved these ends even with primitive technology at their disposal. From the ancient courts of China's first empire to 20th century Nazi and communist regimes, the construction of a police state was made possible by rampant use of spies and informants. But even then, the independent spirit managed to secure occasional moments of privacy, whether in the security of their bedroom reading forbidden literature or in creating secret meeting places where revolutionaries (like Jefferson) plotted to win their freedom back.

> *Modern technology threatens to abolish privacy entirely, often in the name of "protection from enemies."*

Modern technology threatens to abolish privacy entirely, often in the name of "protection from enemies." After all, fear of Irish Republican Army–sponsored terrorism compelled Britain to adopt widespread surveillance in London—just as Washington, D.C., scrambled to install a multitude of cameras despite questions over the effectiveness of these measures and the implications to the freedom of law-abiding citizens. It was the infringement on liberty, in fact, that compelled Jefferson to proclaim that, whenever a form of government becomes destructive to liberty it is the "right of the people to alter or abolish it."

Researchers at the University of California at Berkeley recently determined that the total stockpile of global information doubled between 2000 and 2002. Comprehending the full implications of this estimate is daunting, and foreseeing the future trend of technology may be as difficult today as it was for Jefferson. Certainly the young 21st century will become the most gadget-obsessed, electronically addicted era in history, and there's little doubt that most of these technologies will be *fun*.

We've come a long way from the hunter-gatherer groups which learned to tame fire. Technology has been the reason why because it often makes life more convenient. It turns ordinary human beings into wizards who can harness information from the air the way a medieval alchemist was supposed to be able to turn lead into gold. The *Homo sapiens* species is largely connected through an elaborate webwork of communication; even a person hiking in the Congo can patch into the global network via sat-com phones or global positioning systems. The great diaspora in which humanity was scattered throughout the globe is being stitched into one collective mosaic.

Does this mean that privacy must vanish as we all cram close together? It's an absolutist's argument to ask: "Is technology good or evil?" Obviously the truth lies not in the science itself but in the applications of that science. Utilizing surveillance cameras in a bank to catch a robber might be termed an acceptable use of electronic eyes while having cameras viewing every neighborhood seems threatening.

In the fourth century BCE Plato wrote, "Seeing that everything which has a beginning also has an end, even a constitution such as yours will not last forever, but will in time be dissolved." The chilling prophecy of these words seems especially relevant today as we confront not only legal infringements on constitutionally guaranteed rights but technologies that may do away with these rights altogether. The only solution that suggests itself is to monitor the would-be monitors. If the United States is to remain the bastion of liberty, personal freedom cannot be subject to some giant counting system as every move and thought are monitored. The same cozy web we've created could transform itself into a prison with one large, all-seeing spider at the center.

In such a society a future Jefferson might just be inspired to draft a future declaration. After all, there'll be a lot more at stake than highly taxed tea.

Your Every Move

By Barbara Dority
Humanist, January/February 2004

On November 11, 2003, former President Jimmy Carter condemned U.S. leaders' attacks on American civil liberties, particularly the Uniting and Strengthening America by Providing Appropriate Tools Required to Intercept and Obstruct Terrorism Act (USA Patriot Act). Speaking at a gathering of Human Rights Defenders on the Front Lines of Freedom at the Carter Center in Washington, D.C., Carter said that post–9/11 policies "work against the spirit of human rights" and are "very serious mistakes." Egyptian human rights activist and sociology professor Saad Eddin Ibrahim added, "Every dictator is using what the United States has done under the Patriot Act to justify human rights abuses in the past, as well as a license to continue human rights abuses."

Since its passage in October 2001, the Patriot Act has decimated many basic American civil liberties. The law gives broad new powers to domestic law enforcement and international intelligence agencies. Perhaps worse still, it eliminates the system of checks and balances that gave courts the responsibility of ensuring that these powers weren't abused. The Electronic Frontier Foundation (EFF), an electronic privacy watchdog group, believes that the opportunities for abuse of these broad new powers are immense.

A particularly egregious part of the Patriot Act gives the government access to "any tangible things." This section grants the Federal Bureau of Investigation (FBI) the authority to request an order "requiring the production of any tangible things (including books, records, papers, documents, and other items)" relevant to an investigation of terrorism or clandestine intelligence activities. Although the section is entitled "Access to Certain Business Records," the scope of its authority is far broader and applies to any records pertaining to an individual. This section, which overrides state library confidentiality laws, permits the FBI to compel production of business records, medical records, educational records, and library records without showing probable cause.

Many aspects of the Patriot Act unfairly target immigrants. The attorney general has the ability to "certify" that the government has "reasonable grounds to believe that an alien is a terrorist or is engaged in other activity that endangers the national security of the United States." Once that certification is made and someone is labeled a potential threat, the government may detain him or her indefinitely—based on secret evidence it isn't required to share with anyone.

Currently over 13,000 Arab and Muslim immigrants are being held in deportation proceedings. Not one of them has been charged with terrorism. Most are being deported for routine immigration violations that normally could be rectified in hearings before immigration judges. Families are being separated and lives ruined because of selective enforcement of immigration laws that have been on the books for many years and are now being used to intimidate and deport law-abiding Arab and Muslim Americans. Fear and confusion are pervasive in the Arab-American community today. Many people are too afraid to step forward when they are harassed on the job or fired, when they are denied housing because of their last name, or when a family member is picked up by immigration authorities and detained in another state on evidence that remains undisclosed to both detainees and lawyers alike. According to Karen Rignal's article "Beyond Patriotic" on Alternet.org, some of these people have been detained for as long as eight months, mistreated, and confined 23 hours a day. Some Arab immigrants have opted to return to the Middle East because they no longer feel welcome in the United States.

Fear and confusion are pervasive in the Arab-American community today.

Nearly 700 men are being held at "Camp X-Ray" in Guantanamo Bay, Cuba. But it isn't just "foreigners" who are being deemed dangerous and un-American. For example, there is Tom Treece, a teacher who taught a class on "public issues" at a Vermont high school. A uniformed police officer entered Treece's classroom in the middle of the night because a student art project on the wall showed a picture of Bush with duct tape over his mouth and the words, "Put your duct tape to good use. Shut your mouth." Residents refused to pass the school budget if Treece wasn't fired, resulting in his removal.

The American Civil Liberties Union (ACLU) went to court to help a 15-year-old who faced suspension from school when he refused to take off a T-shirt with the words "International Terrorist" written beneath a picture of Bush. And there was the college student from North Carolina who was visited at home by secret service agents who told her, "Ma'am, we've gotten a report that you have anti-American material." She refused to let them in but eventually showed them what she thought they were after, an anti-death-penalty poster showing Bush and a group of lynched bodies over the epithet "We hang on your every word." The agents then asked her if she had any "pro-Taliban stuff."

Then there's art dealer Doug Stuber, who ran the 2000 North Carolina presidential campaign for Green Party candidate Ralph Nader. Stuber was told he couldn't board a plane to Prague, Czech Republic, because no Greens were allowed to fly that day. He was questioned by police, photographed by two secret service agents, and asked about his family and what the Greens were up to. Stuber reports that he was shown a Justice Department document suggesting that Greens were likely terrorists.

Michael Franti, lead singer of the progressive hip hop band Spearhead, reports that the mother of one of his colleagues, who has a sibling in the Persian Gulf, was visited by "two plain-clothes men from the military" in March 2003. They came in and said, "You have a child who's in the Gulf and you have a child who's in this band Spearhead who's part of the resistance." They had pictures of the band at peace rallies, their flight records for several months, their banking records, and the names of backstage staff.

A report by the ACLU called "Freedom Under Fire" states, "There is a pall over our country. The response to dissent by many government officials so clearly violates the letter and the spirit of the supreme law of the land that they threaten the very underpinnings of democracy itself."

Justice Department spokespeople have repeatedly claimed that the Patriot Act doesn't apply to Americans. But this is false.

In the face of these cases and many more, Justice Department spokespeople have repeatedly claimed that the Patriot Act doesn't apply to Americans. But this is false. First of all, under the Patriot Act the four tools of surveillance—wiretaps, search warrants, pen/trap orders, and subpoenas—are increased. Second, their counterparts under the Foreign Intelligence Surveillance Act (FISA), which allows spying in the United States by foreign intelligence agencies, are concurrently expanded. New definitions of terrorism also increase the amount of government surveillance permitted. And three expansions of previous terms increase the scope of spying allowed. The Patriot Act provides a FISA detour around limitations on federal domestic surveillance and a domestic detour around FISA limitations. The attorney general can nullify domestic surveillance limits on the Central Intelligence Agency, for example, by obtaining a FISA wiretap where probable cause cannot be shown but the person is a suspected foreign government agent. All this information can be shared with the FBI and vice versa.

In sum, the Patriot Act allows U.S. foreign intelligence agencies to more easily spy on U.S. citizens and FISA now provides for increased information sharing between domestic law enforcement and foreign intelligence officials. This partially repeals the protections implemented in the 1970s after the revelation that the FBI and CIA were conducting investigations on thousands of U.S. citizens during and after the McCarthy era. The Patriot Act allows sharing wiretap results and grand jury information when that constitutes "foreign intelligence information."

In response to other criticisms, Justice Department spokespeople have also claimed that the Patriot Act applies only to "terrorists and spies" and that the FBI can't obtain a person's records without probable cause. As one might expect, all of this is false as well.

The Patriot Act specifically gives the government and the FBI authority to monitor people not engaged in criminal activity or espionage and to do so in complete secrecy. It also imposes a gag order that prohibits an organization that has been forced to turn over records from disclosing the fact of the search to its clients, customers, or anyone else.

Furthermore, in other statements, federal officials contradict themselves by saying that the government is using its expanded authority under the far-reaching law to investigate suspected blackmailers, drug traffickers, money launderers, pornographers, and white-collar criminals. Dan Dodson, speaking to the Associated Press this past September on behalf of the National Association of Criminal Defense Attorneys, reported, "Within six months of passing the Patriot Act, the Justice Department was conducting seminars on how to stretch the new wiretapping provisions to extend them beyond terror cases."

A guidebook used in a 2002 Justice Department employee seminar on financial crimes says: "We all know that the USA Patriot Act provided weapons for the war on terrorism. But do you know how it affects the war on crime as well?"

Eric Lichtblau, writing in the September 28, 2003, *New York Times*, reveals that a September report to Congress from the Justice Department "cites more than a dozen cases that are not directly related to terrorism. In them, federal authorities have used their expanded power to investigate individuals, initiate wiretaps and other surveillance, or seize millions in tainted assets." In one case, e-mail and other electronic evidence made possible "the tracking of an unidentified fugitive and an investigation into a computer hacker who stole a company's trade secrets." In other instances, expanded federal authority was used "to investigate a major drug distributor, a four-time killer, an identity thief, and a fugitive who fled on the eve of trial by using a fake passport." The Bureau of Immigration and Customs Enforcement has benefited as well. Lichtblau provides information from a senior official that "investigators in the past two years had seized about $35 million at U.S. borders in undeclared cash, checks, and currency being smuggled out of the country," much of which "involved drug smuggling, corporate fraud, and other nonterrorism crimes." Furthermore, officials in the Justice Department have indicated that the examples cited in the report to Congress are among hundreds of such nonterrorism cases pursued by federal authorities.

Publicly, of course, Attorney General John Ashcroft continues to speak almost exclusively of how Patriot Act powers are helping fight terrorism. In his nationwide tour this past fall to bolster support for the act (which has engendered growing discontent), Ashcroft lauded its "success" stories. However, his department also officially labels many cases as terrorism which aren't. A January 2003 study by the General Accounting Office concluded that, of those convictions classified as "international terrorism," fully 75 percent actually dealt with more common nonterrorist crimes.

Meanwhile, a new bill is quietly circulating on Capitol Hill to give even greater powers to law enforcement—in the name of fighting drug trafficking. The Vital Interdiction of Criminal Terrorist Organizations Act of 2003—or Victory Act—could be introduced in Congress by February 2004. The text of the act was leaked to ABC News and appears to have been prepared by the office of Senator Orin Hatch (Republican, Utah), chair of the Senate Judiciary Committee. This new act includes significant portions of the unpassed, so-called Patriot Act II, which faced broad opposition from conservatives and liberals alike.

And, according to the October 26, 2003, *St. Petersburg Times*, the Bush administration still isn't satisfied and has proposed changes that would "close the loopholes." For example, Bush wants to give the Justice Department the authority to confiscate records and compel testimony without any court or grant jury review. He also wants to chip away at the right to bail. Current law already allows a judge to deny bond for anyone shown to be dangerous or a flight risk, but this isn't good enough for Bush. He is encouraging passage of the "Pretrial Detention and Lifetime Supervision of Terrorists Act of 2003," a bill that would keep people accused of a whole range of new crimes behind bars pending trial by making those crimes "no bond" offenses. This would codify the concept already being used: locking people up first and investigating later. In the aftermath of 9/11, more than 750 immigrants were jailed for many months while the Justice Department looked into potential ties to terrorism—and in the end not one was charged with any crime.

Bush also wants to expand the reach of the federal death penalty by making it applicable to "domestic terrorism." Under the act, *domestic terrorism* is broadly defined as any criminal act intended to influence the government through "intimidation or coercion" involving "dangerous acts." Aggressive protestors of all stripes— from Greenpeace activists to abortion foes—could easily fall within this definition, opening the door for politically motivated executions. Bush also wants passage of the "Antiterrorism Tools Enhancement Act of 2003" (H.R. 3037) and the Anti-Terrorism Intelligence Tools Improvement Act of 2003 (H.R. 3179). Both were proposed in the fall and are now in committee. They would give the FBI "administrative subpoena" authority to confiscate any records and compel any testimony on its authorization alone, thus eliminating court oversight entirely—or as Bush would call it, "interference."

Civil rights and liberties of ordinary U.S. citizens won't be respected. Indeed, should a certain chain of events occur, all one would have to do is donate some money to a group or organization to possibly be linked to terrorism. Consider the following scenario: you send a contribution to Greenpeace. The following week, Greenpeace activists nonviolently blockade an oil tanker coming into New York harbor to protest the company's safety record; however, in the ensuing face-off, a tanker crewmember drowns trying to break the blockade. Under the proposed act's definition of *domestic terrorism*, a prosecutor could charge the Greenpeace protestors with terrorism—and they could face the death penalty. When the prosecutor subpoenas a list of Greenpeace donors, any one of them can be indicted for "material support" of "terrorism" and face a prison term if convicted. This could mean *you*. This isn't as far-fetched as it sounds. Derived from an ACLU analysis, this is just one of many nightmare scenarios possible—and there are worse—if a recently revealed Justice Department draft of new antiterrorism legislation becomes law.

Perhaps the most frightening thing about the Patriot Act . . . is how similar the act is to legislation enacted in the 18th century.

Interestingly, according to the October 27, 2003, Long Island, New York, *Newsday*, the top White House aides who identified an American undercover agent may have committed an act of domestic terrorism as defined in the Patriot Act. Section 802 defines, in part, domestic terrorism as "acts dangerous to human life that are a violation of the criminal laws of the United States or any state that appear to be intended to intimidate or coerce a civilian population." Clearly, disclosing the identity of a CIA undercover agent is an act dangerous to life—the lives of the agent and her contacts abroad whom terrorist groups can now trace—and a violation of the criminal laws of the United States. The obvious intent of the White House in disclosing this classified information was to intimidate the agent's husband, former Ambassador Joseph Wilson, who had become a strong critic of Bush's Iraq policies. And by showing their willingness to make such a dangerous disclosure, officials sent a clear message to all critics that they, too, could be destroyed if they persist. The apparent intention "to intimidate or coerce a civilian population" also meets the act's definition of domestic terrorism. This places the Justice Department investigators in a dilemma: will they treat this investigation differently from others? Under the act, they have acquired expanded powers to wiretap and search—but will they place sweeping and roving wiretaps on

White House aides? Will they engage in secret searches of their offices, computers, and homes? Will they arrest and detain White House aides incommunicado and without access to counsel?

Perhaps the most frightening thing about the Patriot Act—even putting aside these other impending restrictions on civil liberties— is how similar the act is to legislation enacted in the 18th century. The Alien and Sedition Acts are notorious in history for their abuse of basic civil liberties. For example, in 1798, the Alien Friends Act made it lawful for the president of the United States "to order all such aliens, as he shall judge dangerous to the peace and safety of the United States, or shall have reasonable grounds to suspect are concerned in any treasonable or secret machinations against the government thereof, to depart out of the territory of the United States." For years Americans have pointed to legislation like this as a travesty never to be repeated. Yet now it is back!

It seems unimaginable that any presidential administration would impose such brazen attacks as these on the civil liberties of a supposedly free people. Apparently, many Americans were initially so traumatized by 9/11 that they were ready to surrender their most treasured liberties. But pockets of resistance are developing and organizations forming. Three states and more than two hundred cities, counties, and towns around the country have passed resolutions opposing the Patriot Act. Many others are in progress. The language of these resolutions includes statements affirming a commitment to the rights guaranteed in the Constitution and directives to local law enforcement not to cooperate with federal agents involved in investigations deemed unconstitutional. A bill has also been introduced in the House to exclude bookstore and library records from the materials that could be subpoenaed by law enforcement without prior notification of the targeted person.

Some leading organizations, such as the ACLU and EFF, continue to keep the pressure on and are always worthy of support. American citizens who treasure their heritage of freedom should find at least one group to join and support—keeping in mind that the government may one day know the organizations they have checked out.

1984 in 2003?

Fears About the Patriot Act Are Misguided

By Ramesh Ponnuru
National Review, June 2, 2003

Has the war on terrorism become a war on Americans' civil liberties? A coalition of left- and right-wing groups fears so, and has been working hard to restrain the law-and-order impulses of the Bush administration. It's a coalition that includes the ACLU and the American Conservative Union, Nat Hentoff and William Safire, John Conyers and Dick Armey.

The coalition started to form in 1996, when Congress passed an anti-terrorism bill. But it really took off after September 11. Members of the coalition believe that Washington's legislative response—called, rather ludicrously, the "USA Patriot Act," an acronym for "Uniting and Strengthening America by Providing Appropriate Tools to Intercept and Obstruct Terrorism"—was a too-hastily conceived, excessive reaction to the atrocities.

Since then, the coalition has regularly found new cause for alarm. It has protested the administration's plans for military tribunals, the president's designation of "enemy combatants," and the Pentagon's attempts to consolidate data under a program called "Total Information Awareness." This spring, the civil libertarians of left and right worked together again to block Sen. Orrin Hatch's attempt to make permanent those provisions of the Patriot Act which are set to expire next year. They have organized, as well, against the possibility that the Justice Department will propose another dangerous anti-terror bill ("Patriot II").

The civil libertarians have had some success. They forced modifications in the Patriot Act before its enactment. They have inspired some cities to pass resolutions banning their employees from cooperating with federal authorities to implement provisions of the act that violate the Constitution. (Officials in other cities are, presumably, free to violate the Constitution at will.) They imposed legislative restrictions on Total Information Awareness. They have inhibited the administration from proposing anti-terror measures that would generate adverse publicity.

They themselves have gotten favorable publicity. It's an irresistible story for the press: the lion and the lamb lying down together. The press has tended to marvel at the mere existence of the coalition. They have not been quick to note that there is a larger bipartisan coalition on the other side, which is why the civil libertarians have been losing most of the battles. The Patriot Act passed 357–66 in the House and 98–1 in the Senate. In early May, the Senate voted 90–4 to approve another anti-terror provision—making it easier to investigate "lone wolf" terrorists with no proven connection to larger organizations—that the civil libertarians oppose.

More important, the press has not adequately scrutinized the civil libertarians' claims. This has kept the debate mired in platitudes about liberty and security. It has also reduced the incentive for the civil libertarians to do their homework, which has in turn made their case both weaker and more hysterical than it might otherwise have been.

Take the attack on TIPS, the Terrorist Information and Prevention System. This abortive plan would have encouraged truckers, deliverymen, and the like to report suspicious behavior they observed in the course of their work. How effective this idea would have been is open to question. Most of the criticism, however, echoed

---

Of all the measures the administration has adopted, it's the Patriot Act (along with the possible Patriot II) that has inspired the most overheated criticisms.

---

former Republican congressman Bob Barr, who said that TIPS "smacks of the very type of fascist or communist government we fought so hard to eradicate in other countries in decades past."

But of all the measures the administration has adopted, it's the Patriot Act (along with the possible Patriot II) that has inspired the most overheated criticisms. When it was passed, the Electronic Frontier Foundation wrote that "the civil liberties of ordinary Americans have taken a tremendous blow with this law." The ACLU says the law "gives the Executive Branch sweeping new powers that undermine the Bill of Rights." But most of the concerns about Patriot are misguided or based on premises that are just plain wrong.

Roving Wiretaps

Thanks to the Patriot Act, terrorism investigations can use roving wiretaps. Instead of having to get new judicial authorization for each phone number tapped, investigators can tap any phone their target uses. This is important when fighting terrorists whose MO includes frequently switching hotel rooms and cell phones. It's a commonsense measure. It's also nothing new: Congress authorized roving wiretaps in ordinary criminal cases back in 1986. It's hard to see Patriot as a blow to civil liberties on this score.

Internet Surveillance

Libertarians have been particularly exercised about Patriot's green light for "spying on the Web browsers of people who are not even criminal suspects"—to quote *Reason* editor Nick Gillespie. This is a misunderstanding of Patriot, as George Washington University law professor Orin Kerr has demonstrated in a law-review article. Before Patriot, it wasn't clear that any statute limited the government's, or even a private party's, ability to obtain basic information about electronic communications (e.g., to whom you're sending e-mails). Patriot required a court order to get that information, and made it a federal crime to get it without one.

Kerr believes that the bar for getting a court order should be raised. But he notes that Patriot made the privacy protections for the Internet as strong as those for phone calls and stronger than for mail. Patriot's Internet provisions, he concludes, "updated the surveillance laws without substantially shifting the balance between privacy and security."

James Bovard traffics in another Patriot myth in a recent cover story for *The American Conservative*: that it "empowers federal agents to cannibalize Americans' e-mail with Carnivore wiretaps." Carnivore is an Internet surveillance tool designed by the FBI. Don't be scared by the name. The FBI's previous tool was dubbed "Omnivore," and this new one was so named because it would be more selective in acquiring information, getting only what was covered by a court order and leaving other information private. But even if Carnivore is a menace, it's not the fault of Patriot. As Kerr points out, "The only provisions of the Patriot Act that directly address Carnivore are pro-privacy provisions that actually restrict the use of Carnivore."

Hacking

Also in *Reason*, Jesse Walker writes that Patriot "expands the definition of *terrorist* to include such non-lethal acts as computer hacking." That's misleading. Pre-Patriot, an Al Qaeda member who hacked the electric company's computers to take out the grid could not be judged guilty of terrorism, even if he would be so judged if he accomplished the same result with a bomb. Hacking per se isn't terrorism, and Patriot doesn't treat it as such.

Sneak and Peek

The ACLU is running ads that say that Patriot lets the government "secretly enter your home while you're away . . . rifle through your personal belongings . . . download your computer files . . . and seize any items at will." Worst of all, "you may never know what the government has done." Reality check: You will be notified if a sneak-and-peek search has been done, just after the fact—usually within a few days. The feds had the authority to conduct these searches before Patriot. A federal judge has to authorize such a search warrant, and the warrant has to specify what's to be seized.

Library Records

Bovard is appalled that Patriot allows "federal agents to commandeer library records," and the American Library Association shares his sentiment. Patriot doesn't mention libraries specifically, but does authorize terrorism investigators to collect tangible records generally. Law enforcement has, however, traditionally been able to obtain library records with a subpoena. Prof. Kerr suggests that because of Patriot, the privacy of library records may be better protected in terrorism investigations than it is in ordinary criminal ones.

The civil libertarians deserve some credit. Their objections helped to rid Patriot of some provisions—such as a crackdown on Internet gambling—that didn't belong in an anti-terrorism bill. Armey added the Carnivore protections to the bill. The law, as finally enacted, places limits on how much officials may disclose of the information they gain from Internet and phone surveillance. Moreover, the civil libertarians make a reasonable demand when they ask that Patriot be subject to periodic re-authorizations, so that Congress can regularly consider making modifications.

The civil libertarians rarely acknowledge the costs of legal laxity: Restrictions on intelligence gathering may well have impeded the investigation of Zacarias Moussaoui, the "twentieth hijacker," before 9/11. David Cole, one of the movement's favorite law professors, goes so far as to lament that U.S. law makes "mere membership in a terrorist group grounds for exclusion and deportation."

And while civil libertarians may scant the value of Patriot, terrorists do not. Jeffrey Battle, an accused member of a terrorist cell in Portland, complained about Patriot in a recorded phone call that was recently released in court. People were less willing to provide financial support, he said, now that they were more likely to be punished for it.

Speaking of the administration's civil-liberties record, Al Gore said last year that President Bush has "taken the most fateful step in the direction of [a] Big Brother nightmare that any president has ever allowed to occur." Dick Armey worries about "the lust for power that these people in the Department of Justice have." The civil-liberties debate could use a lot less rhetoric of this sort—and a lot more attention to detail.

A calm look at the Patriot Act shows that it's less of a threat to civil liberties than, say, campaign-finance reform. A lot of the controversy is the result of confusion. Opponents of the Patriot Act are fond of complaining that few people have bothered to read it. No kidding.

The Patriot Act Without Tears

By Andrew C. McCarthy
National Review, June 14, 2004

It was mid-August 2001, the last desperate days before the 9/11 terrorist attacks. Desperate, that is, for an alert agent of the FBI's Foreign Counterintelligence Division (FCI); much of the rest of America, and certainly much of the rest of its government, blithely carried on, content to assume, despite the number and increasing ferocity of terrorist attacks dating back nearly nine years, that national security was little more than an everyday criminal-justice issue.

Since 1995, a "wall" had been erected, presumptively barring communications between FCI agents and their counterparts in law enforcement—the FBI's criminal agents and the assistant U.S. attorneys who collectively, after a string of successful prosecutions through the 1990s, had become the government's best resource for information about the threat of militant Islam. This wall was not required by law; it was imposed as policy. Justice Department lawyers, elevating litigation risk over national security, designed it to forestall accusations that the federal government had used its intelligence-eavesdropping authority to build criminal cases.

This FCI agent collided, head-on, with the wall; and strewn in the wreckage was the last, best hope of stopping 9/11. Putting disconnected clues together, the agent had deduced that two Qaeda operatives, Khalid al-Midhar and Nawaf al-Hazmi, had probably gotten into the U.S. Alarmed, he pleaded with the FBI's criminal division to help him hunt down the terrorists—but they refused: For agents to fuse their information and efforts would be a transgression against the wall. The prescient agent rued that, one day soon, people would die in the face of this paralyzing roadblock. Al-Midhar and al-Hazmi remained undetected until they plunged Flight 77 into the Pentagon on 9/11.

Facing Reality

By October 2001, the world had changed—and the USA Patriot Act was passed. So patent was the need for this law that it racked up massive support: 357-66 in the House, 98-1 in the Senate. In the nearly three years since, however, it has been distorted beyond recognition by a coalition of anti-Bush leftists and libertarian extremists, such that it is now perhaps the most broadly maligned—and misunderstood—piece of meaningful legislation in U.S. history. If our nation is serious about national security, the Patriot Act must be made permanent; instead, it could soon be gone—and the disastrous "intelligence wall" rebuilt.

Contrary to widespread calumny, Patriot is not an assault on the Bill of Rights. It is, basically, an overhaul of the government's anti-quated counter-terror arsenal, which had been haplessly fighting a 21st-century war with 20th-century weapons. Indeed, Patriot's only obvious flaw is its cloying acronym, short for "The Uniting and Strengthening America by Providing Appropriate Tools to Intercept and Obstruct Terrorism Act of 2001." But once you get past the title, Patriot is all substance, and crucial to national security.

The most essential improvement wrought by Patriot has been the dismantling of the intelligence wall. The bill expressly amended the government's national-security eavesdrop-ping-and-search authority (under the Foreign Intelligence Surveillance Act or FISA) to clarify that intelligence agents, criminal investigators, and prosecutors not only may but should be pooling information and connecting dots. This is common sense: Along the way toward mass murder, terrorists inevitably commit numerous ordinary crimes, everything from identity theft to immigration fraud to bombing. One could not surveil them as agents of a foreign power (as FISA permits) without necessarily uncovering such crimes, and this, far from being a problem, is a bonus since these lay the groundwork for prosecutions that can both stop terrorists before they strike and pressure them to turn state's evidence.

> *Contrary to widespread calumny, Patriot is not an assault on the Bill of Rights.*

Yet, as has been detailed in a decisive 2002 opinion by the Foreign Intelligence Surveillance Court of Review, FISA had for decades been misinterpreted by the government and the courts, which, owing to their obsession over the "rights" of enemy operatives, erroneously presumed that national-security intelligence was somehow separate and severable from criminal evidence. This false dichotomy culminated in the wall built by the Clinton Justice Department (and substantially maintained by Bush's DOJ), with awful consequences.

Tearing down the wall—as well as repealing legislation that had barred criminal investigators from sharing with intelligence agents the fruits of grand-jury proceedings and criminal wiretaps—has paid instant dividends. For example, while the wall once caused intelligence and criminal agents in Buffalo to believe they could not be in the same room together during briefings to discuss their parallel investigations of an apparent sleeper cell in Lackawanna, N.Y., the Patriot Act allowed the criminal investigators to learn that a theretofore anonymous letter to one of their subjects had, as intelligence agents knew, been penned by a Qaeda operative. This and other fact-sharing broke an investigative logjam, revealing a history of paramilitary training at Al Qaeda's Afghan proving grounds, and directly resulted in guilty pleas and lengthy sentences for six men who had provided material support to the terror network.

In a similar way, in 2002 law-enforcement agents in Oregon learned through an informant that Jeffrey Battle was actively scoping out Jewish schools and synagogues for a terrorist attack. It later emerged that Battle was among a group that set out to train with Al Qaeda in Afghanistan (they never made it). Battle was plainly a time bomb, but his confederates had not yet been fully revealed—and there naturally was fear that if Battle were arrested and removed from the scene the investigators would lose their best hope of identifying other terrorists. Because the wall was down, the criminal investigators had the confidence to delay the arrest and continue the investigation, knowing the intelligence agents using FISA were now free to share what they were learning. As a result, not only Battle but six others, collectively known as the "Portland 7," were identified, convicted on terrorism-support charges, and sentenced to between three and 18 years in prison.

Thanks to Patriot's removal of the blinders, action—sometimes long overdue—has been taken against many other accused and convicted terrorists. Criminal investigators won access to a historic trove of intelligence demonstrating that Prof. Sami al-Arian had been using his University of South Florida redoubt as an annex of the deadly Palestinian Islamic Jihad group responsible for over 100 murders, including that of Alisa Flatow, a young American woman killed in an Israeli bus bombing. The sharing provisions also ensured the convictions of nine other defendants in Virginia, on charges ranging from support of the Qaeda-affiliated Lashkar-e-Taiba to conspiracy to levy war against the U.S.; the conviction in Chicago of bin Laden intimate Enaam Arnaout for using his Benevolence International Foundation as a conduit to fund terrorist cells in Bosnia and Chechnya, and of Khaled Abdel-Latif Dumeisi for working in the U.S. for Saddam Hussein's brutal Iraqi Intelligence Service; the indictment of a University of Idaho graduate student, Sami Omar al-Hussayen, for using his computer skills to support the recruiting and fundraising of Hamas and Chechnyan terror groups; the indictment in Brooklyn of two Yemeni nationals who bragged about having raised millions of dollars for bin Laden; and the smashing of a drugs-for-weapons plot in San Diego that solicited Stinger anti-aircraft missiles for the Taliban in exchange for heroin and hashish. Moreover, while much information provided by criminal investigators to the intelligence community must remain classified, the Justice Department also credits the sharing provisions with the revocation of visas for suspected terrorists, tracking and choking off of terrorist funding channels, and identifying of terrorists operating overseas.

21st-Century Tactics

Besides paving the way for agents to pool critical information, Patriot has been invaluable in modernizing investigative tools to ensure that more information is actually captured. While the critics' persistent caviling misleadingly suggests that these tools are a novel assault on privacy rights, for the most part they merely extend to national-security intelligence investigations the same methods that have long been available to law-enforcement agents probing the vast array of federal crimes, including those as comparatively innocuous as health-care fraud.

Among the best examples is the so-called "roving" (or multipoint) wiretap. As the telephone revolution unfolded, criminals naturally took advantage, avoiding wiretap surveillance by the simple tactic of constantly switching phones—which became especially easy to do once cellphones became ubiquitous. Congress reacted nearly 20 years ago with a law that authorized criminal agents to obtain wiretaps that, rather than aim at a specific telephone, targeted *persons*, thus allowing monitoring to continue without significant delay as criminals ditched one phone for the next. Inexplicably, this same authority was not available to intelligence agents investigating terrorists under FISA. Patriot rectifies this anomaly.

On the law-enforcement side, Patriot expands the substance of the wiretap statute to account for the realities of terrorism. Most Americans would probably be surprised to learn that while the relatively trivial offense of gambling, for example, was a lawful predicate for a criminal wiretap investigation, chemical-weapons offenses, the use of weapons of mass destruction, the killing of Americans abroad, terrorist financing, and computer fraud were not. Thanks to Patriot, that is no longer the case.

Analogously, Patriot revamped other telecommunications-related techniques. Prior law, for example, had been written in the bygone era when cable service meant television programming. Owing to privacy concerns about viewing habits, which the government rarely has a legitimate reason to probe, federal law made access to cable-usage records practically impossible—creating in service providers a fear of being sued by customers if they complied with government information requests. Now, of course, millions of cable subscribers—including no small number of terrorists—use the service not only for entertainment viewing but for e-mail services.

While e-mail-usage records from dial-up providers have long been available by subpoena, court order, or search warrant (depending on the sensitivity of the information sought), cable providers for years delayed complying with such processes, arguing that their services fell under the restrictive umbrella of prior cable law. This was not only a potentially disastrous state of affairs in terrorism cases, where delay can cost lives, but in many other contexts as well—including one reported case in which a cable company declined to comply with an order to disclose the name of a suspected pedophile who was distributing child pornography on the Internet even as he bragged online about sexually abusing a young girl. (Investigators, forced to pursue other leads, needed two extra weeks to identify and apprehend the suspect.) Recognizing that it made no sense to have radically different standards for acquiring the same information, Patriot made cable e-mail available on the same terms as dial-up.

Patriot also closed other gaping e-mail loopholes. Under prior law, for example, investigators trying to identify the source of incriminating e-mail were severely handicapped in that their readiest tool, the grand-jury subpoena, could be used only to compel the service provider to produce customers' names, addresses, and lengths of service—information often of little value in ferreting out wrongdoers who routinely use false names and temporary e-mail addresses. Patriot solved this problem by empowering grand juries to compel payment information, which can be used to trace the bank and credit-card records by which investigators ultimately establish identity. This not only makes it possible to identify potential terrorists far more quickly—and thus, it is hoped, before they can strike—but also to thwart other criminals who must be apprehended with all due speed. Such subpoenas, for example, have been employed repeatedly to identify and arrest molesters who were actively abusing children. The Justice Department reports that, only a few weeks ago, the new authority prevented a Columbine-like attack by allowing agents to identify a suspect, and obtain his confession, before the attack could take place.

Further, Patriot clarified such investigative matters as the methods for lawful access by investigators to stored e-mail held by third parties (such as AOL and other service providers). And it cured the incongruity that allowed agents to access voice messages stored in a suspect's own home answering machine by a simple search warrant but anomalously forced them to obtain a far more cumbersome wiretap order if the messages were in the form of voicemail stored with a third-party provider.

A Library of Red Herrings

One Patriot reform that has been irresponsibly maligned is Section 215 of the act, which merely extends to national-security investigations conducted under FISA the same authority to subpoena business records that criminal investigators have exercised unremarkably for years. Indeed, even under Section 215, intelligence agents remain at a comparative disadvantage since they must get the approval of a FISA court before compelling records production while prosecutors in criminal cases simply issue grand-jury subpoenas. Nonetheless, this commonsense provision came under blistering, disingenuous assault last year when the ACLU and others raised the red herring of library records—which are not even mentioned in the statute. In 2002, for example, the

Hartford Courant was compelled to retract in full a story that falsely accused the FBI of installing software on computers in the Hartford Public Library to monitor the public's use of the Internet. (In fact, the FBI had obtained a court-ordered search warrant to copy the hard drive of a single computer that had been used criminally to hack into a business computer system in California.)

In 2003, the ACLU issued a warning that Section 215 would allow federal "thought police" to "target us for what we choose to read or what Websites we visit." In reality, Section 215 (unlike criminal-grand-jury subpoena authority) expressly contains safeguards protecting First Amendment rights, and further provides that the attorney general must, twice a year, "fully inform" Congress about how the provision has been implemented. As of September 2003, the provision had not been used a single time—neither for library records nor, indeed, for records of any kind.

Unlike reading habits, financing—the lifeblood of terrorist networks—actually is a Patriot target. The act has significantly crimped the ability of overseas terrorists to use foreign banks and

---

Unlike reading habits, financing—the lifeblood of terrorist networks—actually is a Patriot target.

---

nominees to avoid seizures of their funds; it cracked down on the so-called "hawalas" (that is, unlicensed money-transmitting businesses) that have been used to funnel millions of dollars to terror groups; it extended the reach of civil money-laundering penalties—which loom large in the minds of financial institutions—against those who engage in transactions involving the proceeds of crime. And it further choked the funding channels by making currency smuggling itself (rather than the mere failure to file a report about the movement of currency) a crime, an initiative that bolsters the legal basis for seizing all, rather than a portion, of the smuggled funds. These and other Patriot finance provisions have enabled the government to obtain over 20 convictions to date and freeze over $130 million in assets worldwide.

Mention should also be made of another Patriot improvement that has been speciously challenged: the codification of uniform procedures for so-called sneak-and-peek warrants, which allow agents to conduct a search without seizing items, and delay notification to the person whose premises have been searched—thus ensuring that an investigation can proceed and agents can continue identifying other conspirators. Such warrants have been used for many years, and delayed notification has been commonplace—just as it is in other areas, such as wiretap law, where alerting the subject would prematurely end the investigation.

Sneak-and-peek delayed notification, however, evolved through federal case law rather than by statute, and consequently there was a jumble to varying requirements depending on which federal circuit the investigation happened to be in. All Patriot did in this regard was impose a uniform national standard that permits delay if notification could cause endangerment to life, facilitation of flight, destruction of evidence, intimidation of witnesses, or similar substantial jeopardizing of investigations. Yet critics drummed up outrage by portraying sneak-and-peek as if it were a novel encroachment on privacy rather than a well-established tool that requires prior court approval. So effective was this campaign that the House of Representatives responded by voting to deny funding for the delayed-notification warrants. Inability to delay notification, of course, would defeat the purpose of using sneak-and-peek in the first place. The Senate has not seemed inclined to follow suit, but that so prudent a provision could become the subject of controversy illustrates how effectively the opposition has discredited the Patriot Act.

Palpably, the Patriot Act, far from imperiling the Constitution, went a long way toward shoring up the perilous state of national security that existed on the morning of 9/11. That is why it is so excruciating to note that, despite all we have been through, we will be transported right back to that precarious state if Congress fails to reauthorize Patriot. Because of intense lobbying by civil-liberties groups instinctively hostile to anything that makes government stronger—even in the arena of national defense, where we need it to be strong if we are to have liberties at all—Patriot's sponsors had to agree, to secure passage, that the act would effectively be experimental. That is, the information sharing, improved investigative techniques, and several other provisions were not permanently enacted into law but are scheduled to "sunset" on December 31, 2005. Dismayingly, far from grasping the eminent sense in making these improvements permanent, the alliance of Democratic Bush-bashers and crusading Republican libertarians is actually pushing a number of proposals to *extend* the sunset provision to parts of Patriot that were not originally covered.

At a time when the 9/11 Commission public hearings highlight intelligence lapses and investigative backwardness—and when Al Qaeda publicly threatens larger-than-ever attacks while continuing to fight our forces and allies on the battlefield and in murderous attacks throughout the world—it is remarkable that elected officials would have *any* priority other than making the Patriot Act permanent.

Appendix

Relevant Amendments to the U.S. Constitution

First Amendment:

Congress shall make no law respecting an establishment of religion, or prohibiting the free exercise thereof; or abridging the freedom of speech, or of the press; or the right of the people peaceably to assemble, and to petition the Government for a redress of grievances.

Fourth Amendment:

The right of the people to be secure in their persons, houses, papers, and effects, against unreasonable searches and seizures, shall not be violated, and no Warrants shall issue, but upon probable cause, supported by Oath or affirmation, and particularly describing the place to be searched, and the persons or things to be seized.

Fifth Amendment:

No person shall be held to answer for a capital, or otherwise infamous crime, unless on a presentment or indictment of a Grand Jury, except in cases arising in the land or naval forces, or in the Militia, when in actual service in time of War or public danger; nor shall any person be subject for the same offense to be twice put in jeopardy of life or limb; nor shall be compelled in any criminal case to be a witness against himself, nor be deprived of life, liberty, or property, without due process of law; nor shall private property be taken for public use, without just compensation.

Sixth Amendment:

In all criminal prosecutions, the accused shall enjoy the right to a speedy and public trial, by an impartial jury of the State and district wherein the crime shall have been committed, which district shall have been previously ascertained by law, and to be informed of the nature and cause of the accusation; to be confronted with the witnesses against him; to have compulsory process for obtaining witnesses in his favor, and to have the Assistance of Counsel for his defense.

Fourteenth Amendment:

Section 1. All persons born or naturalized in the United States and subject to the jurisdiction thereof, are citizens of the United States and of the State wherein they reside. No State shall make or enforce any law which shall abridge the privileges or immunities of citizens of the United States; nor shall any State deprive any person of life, liberty, or property, without due process of law; nor deny to any person within its jurisdiction the equal protection of the laws.

Section 2. Representatives shall be apportioned among the several States according to their respective numbers, counting the whole number of persons in each State, excluding Indians not taxed. But when the right to vote at any election for the choice of electors for President and Vice President of the United States, Representatives in Congress, the Executive and Judicial officers of a State, or the members of the Legislature thereof, is denied to any of the male inhabitants of such State, being 21 years of age, and citizens of the United States, or in any way abridged, except for participation in rebellion, or other crime, the basis of representation therein shall be reduced in the proportion which the number of such male citizens shall bear to the whole number of male citizens 21 years of age in such State.

Section 3. No person shall be a Senator or Representative in Congress, or elector of President and Vice President, or hold any office, civil or military, under the United States, or under any State, who, having previously taken an oath, as a member of Congress, or as an officer of the United States, or as a member of any State legislature, or as an executive or judicial officer of any State, to support the Constitution of the United States, shall have engaged in insurrection or rebellion against the same, or given aid or comfort to the enemies thereof. But Congress may, by a vote of two-thirds of each House, remove such disability.

Section 4. The validity of the public debt of the United States, authorized by law, including debts incurred for payment of pensions and bounties for services in suppressing insurrection or rebellion, shall not be questioned. But neither the United States nor any State shall assume or pay any debt or obligation incurred in aid of insurrection or rebellion against the United States, or any claim for the loss or emancipation of any slave; but all such debts, obligations, and claims shall be held illegal and void.

Section 5. The Congress shall have power to enforce, by appropriate legislation, the provisions of this article.

The Universal Declaration of Human Rights

Adopted by the General Assembly of the United Nations as Resolution 217A (III) on December 10, 1948.

Preamble

Whereas recognition of the inherent dignity and of the equal and inalienable rights of all members of the human family is the foundation of freedom, justice, and peace in the world,

Whereas disregard and contempt for human rights have resulted in barbarous acts which have outraged the conscience of mankind, and the advent of a world in which human beings shall enjoy freedom of speech and belief and freedom from fear and want has been proclaimed as the highest aspiration of the common people,

Whereas it is essential, if man is not to be compelled to have recourse, as a last resort, to rebellion against tyranny and oppression, that human rights should be protected by the rule of law,

Whereas it is essential to promote the development of friendly relations between nations,

Whereas the peoples of the United Nations have in the Charter reaffirmed their faith in fundamental human rights, in the dignity and worth of the human person, and in the equal rights of men and women and have determined to promote social progress and better standards of life in larger freedom,

Whereas Member States have pledged themselves to achieve, in co-operation with the United Nations, the promotion of universal respect for and observance of human rights and fundamental freedoms,

Whereas a common understanding of these rights and freedoms is of the greatest importance for the full realization of this pledge,

Now, Therefore THE GENERAL ASSEMBLY proclaims THIS UNIVERSAL DECLARATION OF HUMAN RIGHTS as a common standard of achievement for all peoples and all nations, to the end that every individual and every organ of society, keeping this Declaration constantly in mind, shall strive by teaching and education to promote respect for these rights and freedoms and by progressive measures, national and international, to secure their universal and effective recognition and observance, both among the peoples of Member States themselves and among the peoples of territories under their jurisdiction.

Article 1

All human beings are born free and equal in dignity and rights. They are endowed with reason and conscience and should act towards one another in a spirit of brotherhood.

Article 2

Everyone is entitled to all the rights and freedoms set forth in this Declaration, without distinction of any kind, such as race, colour, sex, language, religion, political or other opinion, national or social origin, property, birth, or other status. Furthermore, no distinction shall be made on the basis of the political, jurisdictional, or international status of the country or territory to which a person belongs, whether it be independent, trust, non-self-governing, or under any other limitation of sovereignty.

Article 3
Everyone has the right to life, liberty, and security of person.

Article 4
No one shall be held in slavery or servitude; slavery and the slave trade shall be prohibited in all their forms.

Article 5
No one shall be subjected to torture or to cruel, inhuman, or degrading treatment or punishment.

Article 6
Everyone has the right to recognition everywhere as a person before the law.

Article 7
All are equal before the law and are entitled without any discrimination to equal protection of the law. All are entitled to equal protection against any discrimination in violation of this Declaration and against any incitement to such discrimination.

Article 8
Everyone has the right to an effective remedy by the competent national tribunals for acts violating the fundamental rights granted him by the constitution or by law.

Article 9
No one shall be subjected to arbitrary arrest, detention, or exile.

Article 10
Everyone is entitled in full equality to a fair and public hearing by an independent and impartial tribunal, in the determination of his rights and obligations and of any criminal charge against him.

Article 11
1. Everyone charged with a penal offence has the right to be presumed innocent until proved guilty according to law in a public trial at which he has had all the guarantees necessary for his defence.
2. No one shall be held guilty of any penal offence on account of any act or omission which did not constitute a penal offence, under national or international law, at the time when it was committed. Nor shall a heavier pen-

alty be imposed than the one that was applicable at the time the penal offence was committed.

Article 12

No one shall be subjected to arbitrary interference with his privacy, family, home, or correspondence, nor to attacks upon his honour and reputation. Everyone has the right to the protection of the law against such interference or attacks.

Article 13

1. Everyone has the right to freedom of movement and residence within the borders of each state.
2. Everyone has the right to leave any country, including his own, and to return to his country.

Article 14

1. Everyone has the right to seek and to enjoy in other countries asylum from persecution.
2. This right may not be invoked in the case of prosecutions genuinely arising from non-political crimes or from acts contrary to the purposes and principles of the United Nations.

Article 15

1. Everyone has the right to a nationality.
2. No one shall be arbitrarily deprived of his nationality nor denied the right to change his nationality.

Article 16

1. Men and women of full age, without any limitation due to race, nationality, or religion, have the right to marry and to found a family. They are entitled to equal rights as to marriage, during marriage and at its dissolution.
2. Marriage shall be entered into only with the free and full consent of the intending spouses.
3. The family is the natural and fundamental group unit of society and is entitled to protection by society and the State.

Article 17

1. Everyone has the right to own property alone as well as in association with others.
2. No one shall be arbitrarily deprived of his property.

Article 18

Everyone has the right to freedom of thought, conscience, and religion; this right includes freedom to change his religion or belief, and freedom, either alone or in community with others and in public or private, to manifest his religion or belief in teaching, practice, worship, and observance.

Article 19

Everyone has the right to freedom of opinion and expression; this right includes freedom to hold opinions without interference and to seek, receive, and impart information and ideas through any media and regardless of frontiers.

Article 20

1. Everyone has the right to freedom of peaceful assembly and association.
2. No one may be compelled to belong to an association.

Article 21

1. Everyone has the right to take part in the government of his country, directly or through freely chosen representatives.
2. Everyone has the right of equal access to public service in his country.
3. The will of the people shall be the basis of the authority of government; this will shall be expressed in periodic and genuine elections which shall be by universal and equal suffrage and shall be held by secret vote or by equivalent free voting procedures.

Article 22

Everyone, as a member of society, has the right to social security and is entitled to realization, through national effort and international co-operation and in accordance with the organization and resources of each State, of the economic, social, and cultural rights indispensable for his dignity and the free development of his personality.

Article 23

1. Everyone has the right to work, to free choice of employment, to just and favourable conditions of work, and to protection against unemployment.
2. Everyone, without any discrimination, has the right to equal pay for equal work.
3. Everyone who works has the right to just and favourable remuneration ensuring for himself and his family an existence worthy of human dignity, and supplemented, if necessary, by other means of social protection.
4. Everyone has the right to form and to join trade unions for the protection of his interests.

Article 24

Everyone has the right to rest and leisure, including reasonable limitation of working hours and periodic holidays with pay.

Article 25

1. Everyone has the right to a standard of living adequate for the health and well-being of himself and of his family, including food, clothing, housing, and medical care and necessary social services, and the right to security in the event of unemployment, sickness, disability, widowhood, old age, or other lack of livelihood in circumstances beyond his control.

2. Motherhood and childhood are entitled to special care and assistance. All children, whether born in or out of wedlock, shall enjoy the same social protection.

Article 26

1. Everyone has the right to education. Education shall be free, at least in the elementary and fundamental stages. Elementary education shall be compulsory. Technical and professional education shall be made generally available and higher education shall be equally accessible to all on the basis of merit.

2. Education shall be directed to the full development of the human personality and to the strengthening of respect for human rights and fundamental freedoms. It shall promote understanding, tolerance, and friendship among all nations, racial, or religious groups, and shall further the activities of the United Nations for the maintenance of peace.

3. Parents have a prior right to choose the kind of education that shall be given to their children.

Article 27

1. Everyone has the right freely to participate in the cultural life of the community, to enjoy the arts, and to share in scientific advancement and its benefits.

2. Everyone has the right to the protection of the moral and material interests resulting from any scientific, literary, or artistic production of which he is the author.

Article 28

Everyone is entitled to a social and international order in which the rights and freedoms set forth in this Declaration can be fully realized.

Article 29

1. Everyone has duties to the community in which alone the free and full development of his personality is possible.

2. In the exercise of his rights and freedoms, everyone shall be subject only to such limitations as are determined by law solely for the purpose of securing due recognition and respect for the rights and freedoms of others and of meeting the just requirements of morality, public order, and the general welfare in a democratic society.

3. These rights and freedoms may in no case be exercised contrary to the purposes and principles of the United Nations.

Article 30

Nothing in this Declaration may be interpreted as implying for any State, group, or person any right to engage in any activity or to perform any act aimed at the destruction of any of the rights and freedoms set forth herein.

The Defense of Marriage Act

One Hundred Fourth Congress of the United States of America

At the Second Session

Begun and held at the City of Washington on Wednesday, the third day of January, one thousand nine hundred and ninety-six

An Act
To define and protect the institution of marriage.

> Be it enacted by the Senate and House of Representatives of the United States of America in Congress assembled,

Section 1. Short Title
This Act may be cited as the "Defense of Marriage Act."

Section 2. Powers Reserved to the States
(a) In General—Chapter 115 of title 28, United States Code, is amended by adding after section 1738B the following:

> "Sec. 1738C. Certain acts, records, and proceedings and the effect thereof

> "No State, territory, or possession of the United States, or Indian tribe, shall be required to give effect to any public act, record, or judicial proceeding of any other State, territory, possession, or tribe respecting a relationship between persons of the same sex that is treated as a marriage under the laws of such other State, territory, possession, or tribe, or a right or claim arising from such relationship."

(b) Clerical Amendment—The table of sections at the beginning of chapter 115 of title 28, United States Code, is amended by inserting after the item relating to section 1738B the following new item:

> "1738C. Certain acts, records, and proceedings and the effect thereof."

Section 3. Definition of Marriage
(a) In General—Chapter 1 of title 1, United States Code, is amended by adding at the end the following:

> "Sec. 7. Definition of 'marriage' and 'spouse'

> "In determining the meaning of any Act of Congress, or of any ruling, regulation, or interpretation of the various administrative bureaus and agencies of the United States, the word 'marriage' means only a legal union between one man and one woman as husband and wife, and the word 'spouse' refers only to a person of the opposite sex who is a husband or a wife."

(b) Clerical Amendment—The table of sections at the beginning of chapter 1 of title 1, United States Code, is amended by inserting after the item relating to section 6 the following new item:

"7. Definition of 'marriage' and 'spouse.'"

Speaker of the House of Representatives.
Vice President of the United States and President of the Senate.

Bibliography

Books

Balkin, Jack M. *What* Roe v. Wade *Should Have Said: The Nation's Top Legal Experts Rewrite America's Most Controversial Decision*. New York: New York University Press, 2005.

Ball, Howard. *The Supreme Court in the Intimate Lives of Americans: Birth, Sex, Marriage, Childrearing, and Death*. New York: New York University Press, 2002.

Ball, Howard. *The USA Patriot Act of 2001: Balancing Civil Liberties and National Security: A Reference Handbook*. Santa Barbara, CA: ABC-CLIO, 2004.

Chang, Nancy. *Silencing Political Dissent: How Post–September 11 Anti-Terrorism Measures Threaten Our Civil Liberties*. New York: Seven Stories Press/Open Media, 2002.

Cohen, David B., and John W. Wells, eds. *American National Security and Civil Liberties in an Era of Terrorism*. New York: Palgrave Macmillan, 2004.

Cole, David. *Enemy Aliens: Immigrants' Rights and American Freedoms in the War on Terrorism*. New York: New Press, 2003.

Cole, David, and James X. Dempsey. *Terrorism and the Constitution: Sacrificing Civil Liberties in the Name of National Security*. New York: New Press, 2002.

Etzioni, Amitai. *How Patriotic Is the Patriot Act?: Freedom Versus Security in the Age of Terrorism*. New York: Routledge, 2004.

Foner, Eric. *The Story of American Freedom*. New York: W.W. Norton & Company, 1998.

Garrow, David J. *Liberty and Sexuality: The Right to Privacy and the Making of* Roe V. Wade. New York: Macmillan, 1994.

Gerstmann, Evan. *Same-Sex Marriage and the Constitution*. New York: Cambridge University Press, 2003.

Goldberg, Danny, Victor Goldberg, and Robert Greenwald, eds. *It's a Free Country: Personal Freedom in America After September 11*. New York: Nation Books/Thunder's Mouth Press, 2003.

Gottfried, Ted. *Homeland Security Versus Constitutional Rights*. Brookfield, CT: 21st Century Books, 2003.

Hull, N. E. H., and Peter Charles Hoffer. Roe v. Wade*: The Abortion Rights Controversy in American History*. Lawrence, KS: University Press of Kansas, 2001.

Linfield, Michael. *Freedom Under Fire: U.S. Civil Liberties in Times of War*. Boston: South End Press, 1990.

Leone, Richard C., and Greg Anrig, Jr., eds. *The War on Our Freedoms: Civil Liberties in an Age of Terrorism*. New York: BBS Public Affairs, 2003.

McClosky, Herbert, and Alida Brill. *Dimensions of Tolerance: What Americans Believe About Civil Liberties*. New York: Russell Sage, 1983.

Ojeda, Auriana, ed. *Should Abortion Rights Be Restricted?* San Diego, CA: Greenhaven Press, 2003.

Rehnquist, William H. *All the Laws But One: Civil Liberties in Wartime*. New York: Knopf, 1998.

Schulhofer, Stephen J. *The Enemy Within: Intelligence Gathering, Law Enforcement, and Civil Liberties in the Wake of September 11*. New York: Century Foundation, 2002.

Smith, Norris, and Lynn M. Messina, eds. *Homeland Security*. New York: H.W. Wilson, 2004.

Sprigg, Peter. *Outrage: How Gay Activists and Liberal Judges Are Trashing Democracy to Redefine Marriage*. Washington, D.C.: Regnery Publishing, 2004.

Steven, Graeme C. S., and Rohan Gunaratna. *Counterterrorism: A Reference Handbook*. Santa Barbara, CA: ABC-CLIO, 2004.

Stone, Geoffrey R. *Perilous Times: Free Speech in Wartime from the Sedition Act of 1798 to the War on Terrorism*. New York: W.W. Norton & Company, 2004.

Sullivan, Andrew. *Same-Sex Marriage: Pro and Con: A Reader*. New York: Vintage Books, 1997.

Walker, Samuel. *Civil Liberties in America: A Reference Handbook*. Santa Barbara, CA: ABC-CLIO, 2004.

Wolfson, Evan. *Why Marriage Matters: America, Equality, and Gay People's Right to Marry*. New York: Simon & Schuster, 2004.

Web Sites

Readers seeking additional information about civil liberties in the United States may wish to refer to the following Web sites, all of which were operational as of this writing.

American Civil Liberties Union

www.aclu.org

This is the official Web site of the American Civil Liberties Union (ACLU), a nonpartisan, nonprofit organization dedicated to defending and preserving the individual rights and liberties of U.S. citizens.

Amnesty International USA

www.amnestyusa.org

Amnesty International (AI) is a nonprofit organization that conducts research and activities focused on preserving and promoting human rights. AI also works to prevent such human rights violations as physical and mental abuse, suppressions of individual freedoms, and various forms of discrimination. Amnesty International USA (AIUSA) is AI's U.S. division.

Center for Democracy & Technology

www.cdt.org

The Center for Democracy and Technology (CDT) is an activist group that seeks to defend privacy and free expression on the Internet and within the framework of other communications technologies. This Web site offers news on various issues related to the intersection of civil liberties and technology, links to relevant articles, and an archive of Congressional testimony and speeches.

Department of Homeland Security

www.dhs.gov/dhspublic

This is the official home page of the Department of Homeland Security. The Web site provides an overview of the structure, organization, and operations of the department; news about defense measures; security advisories; and information bulletins.

First Amendment Center

www.firstamendmentcenter.org

This site offers access to a wide range of information about the First Amendment and related issues, including background information, daily news, analysis, and commentary. The Center is a nonprofit organization affiliated with Vanderbilt University, in Nashville, Tennessee, and the Newseum, in Arlington, Virginia.

Libertystory.net
www.libertystory.net

Maintained by the historian Jim Powell, a senior fellow at the Cato Institute, Libertystory.net is dedicated to supplying information about ideas, people, and events that have shaped the history of liberty, both in the United States and abroad. The Web site is updated weekly.

USA PATRIOT Act—Electronic Privacy Information Center (EPIC)
www.epic.org/privacy/terrorism/hr3162.html

This site offers the full text of the USA PATRIOT Act, passed on October 24, 2001. EPIC, a public interest research center established in 1994 and based in Washington, D.C., seeks to focus public attention on civil liberties issues and defend individual privacy, the First Amendment, and the principles of the U.S. Constitution.

The White House—Homeland Security
www.whitehouse.gov/homeland

This section of the official White House Web site presents links to news and press releases about homeland security, as well as general information about various government security initiatives.

Additional Periodical Articles with Abstracts

More information and perspectives on the subject of U.S. civil liberties can be found in the following articles. Readers who require a more comprehensive selection of articles are advised to consult the *Readers' Guide to Periodical Literature* and other H.W. Wilson publications.

What Can You Do? John Caldwell. *The Advocate*, p31 March 30, 2004.

Caldwell offers advice and strategies for those wishing to oppose President Bush's endorsement of a proposed constitutional amendment to ban same-sex marriage.

PATRIOT Act Games. Bob Barr. *The American Spectator*, v. 36 pp34–35 August/September 2003.

According to Barr, the USA PATRIOT Act of 2001 allows for an unprecedented expansion of federal law-enforcement powers that, through marginal security increases, significantly diminish the civil liberties of U.S. citizens. Left unchecked, the act threatens the constitutional assertion that citizens have rights over their persons and property unless there is a sound, articulated, and specific reason for the government to interfere. Barr points out that the terrorists responsible for the attacks of September 11, 2001, were in the U.S. illegally or had overstayed their lawful presence; in other words, the government could have identified and stopped them before the attacks, but failed to do so. In the author's view, the proper way to catch such terrorists is with better intelligence gathering, better coordination and analysis, better use of existing policing tools, and more rapid and appropriate dissemination of intelligence. However, the USA PATRIOT Act, Barr asserts, is a legislative mess that does little to encourage better law enforcement and intelligence work.

Artist Ensnared by Patriot Act. Stephanie Cash. *Art in America*, v. 92 p35 September 2004.

Cash relates the story of the Buffalo, New York–based artist Steve Kurtz, who became the subject of a highly publicized federal investigation in 2004. On May 11, Kurtz awoke to find his wife dead beside him. Emergency workers arriving on the scene discovered items in Kurtz's home that they considered suspicious and contacted the FBI. Kurtz, a member of the radical artists' collective known as Critical Art Ensemble (CAE), had obtained laboratory equipment and two strains of harmless bacterial material for an art project. Invoking a 1989 bioterrorism law and the PATRIOT Act, federal agents detained the artist for 22 hours and seized his possessions for a week, until it was determined that his wife's heart failure was unrelated to the bacterial matter.

On Abortion: A Lincolnian Position. George McKenna. *The Atlantic Monthly*, v. 276 pp51–54+ September 1995.

According to McKenna, Abraham Lincoln's position on slavery offers a model for a new political approach to abortion. Lincoln took issue with defenders of states' or territories' rights to permit slavery who argued—much as defenders of abortion rights do today—that opposition to the practice was essentially religious or private and had no place in a constitutional debate. At the same time, he did not try to abolish slavery. Instead, he depicted slavery as a moral cancer that could be eliminated only if it were first contained. A similar approach to abortion, McKenna suggests, would accept the procedure's legality but not its moral legitimacy, treating it as a wrong without demanding an immediate end to it. Such an approach would focus on restricting and discouraging abortion, supporting the quest for alternatives, and building public consensus for an ultimate end to the practice.

Rights, Liberties, and Security: Civil Rights and National Security in Post–9/11 America. Stuart Taylor, Jr. *Brookings Review*, v. 21 pp25–31 Winter 2003.

The author argues that the urgency of infiltrating clandestine terrorist cells makes it essential that Congress undertake a candid and systematic reassessment of the civil liberties that hinder the government's power to investigate and detain. The United States is being confronted by an unprecedented danger: a mass movement of militant Islamic terrorists determined to kill as many of their perceived enemies as possible. Ultimately, according to Taylor, the number of casualties can be kept to a minimum only by imprisoning or killing potential Al Qaeda terrorists who plan to infiltrate the United States and avoid attention until they attack. In the author's view, serious national debate and deliberate congressional action should replace what has so far been a largely improvisational approach to terror on the part of the government.

Above the Law. Gregory Magarian. *Commonweal*, v. 131 pp12–13 June 18, 2004.

Magarian discusses two groups of cases in the U.S. Supreme Court in 2004 that challenge the government's imprisonment of alleged "enemy combatants." Although these cases present complex and even arcane questions of law, they ultimately rest on a simple and extremely important question of democratic principle: to what extent the president can be trusted to carry out military affairs without any legal check or oversight. The writer addresses both groups of cases and contends that they provide the Supreme Court with an opportunity to make it clear that the president, even in his capacity as wartime leader, does not have unchecked power to deny U.S. citizens or those under U.S. control their basic legal protections.

Civil Liberties and the War on Terrorism. *Congressional Digest*, v. 83 p257 November 2004.

According to the authors, the U.S. government's response to the terrorist attacks of September 11, 2001, has tested the nation's core freedoms. The PATRIOT Act, which President Bush signed weeks after the attacks, has been controversial from the start, with some claiming that it infringes on constitutional rights and others arguing that it helps protect citizens from potential terrorist attacks. The act will expire in 2005, so it will be the responsibility of Congress to review its value and effectiveness and to reconsider the extent to which U.S. citizens must sacrifice their civil liberties in return for their safety.

Regime Change. Lewis H. Lapham. *Harper's*, v. 306 pp34+ February 2003.

Lapham, the editor of *Harper's* magazine, castigates the Bush administration for ignoring civil liberties, and U.S. citizens for tamely acquiescing in the face of misuses of government power.

Defender of the Free World. Rob Gurwitt. *Mother Jones*, v. 29 pp22–23 January/February 2004.

Gurwitt writes that the USA PATRIOT Act, passed in October 2001, contains language in Section 215 that makes it easier for federal agents to search the business records of, among other places, libraries and bookstores. The act stipulates that agents are no longer required to show probable cause before receiving a judge's approval to obtain private records; the act also makes it illegal for the keeper of those records to inform anyone else, including the customer or patron involved, about the investigation. The writer discusses the growing opposition to Section 215 among librarians, and in particular the work of Trina Magi, a librarian at the University of Vermont's Bailey/Howe Library, who has highlighted the issue in Vermont.

Business Blacklists. Michael Scherer. *Mother Jones*, v. 28 pp17–18 May/June 2003.

Scherer reports that the racial profiling of consumers has become more common since September 11, 2001, as the federal government increasingly requires private enterprises to do the work of law enforcement. Two weeks after the terrorist attacks, President Bush issued an executive order extending sanctions already applied to banks to all businesses, and his administration began adding the names of hundreds of suspected terrorists to the U.S. Treasury's Office of Foreign Asset Control (OFAC) list. In addition, the USA PATRIOT Act of October 2001 requires financial institutions to check every new customer against OFAC's online database, which contains thousands of names and aliases, and federal officials are drafting rules that would mandate customer screening at casinos, insurance companies, car dealerships, travel agencies, pawnbrokers, and gem dealers. In 2002 businesses requested that the Treasury office investigate over 45,000 customers. The writer discusses the negative effects of the OFAC list on innocent people with names that have been appropriated by suspected terrorists.

At First Glance. John Derbyshire. *National Review*, v. 53 pp42–44 October 5, 2001.

Derbyshire argues that racial profiling is a practical and acceptable tool for preventing crime and terrorism. According to the author, the United States can and should use racial profiling to target potential terrorists in high-risk areas such as airports. Although the process is not infallible, Derbyshire maintains, it is a useful aid in identifying possible threats to U.S. citizens.

See No Evil. John O'Sullivan. *National Review*, v. 56 pp22+ December 27, 2004.

O'Sullivan argues that the U.S. government has proved lax in enforcing sensible precautions against further terrorist attacks and is preventing other organizations, notably airlines, from defending public safety as best they can. For example, the Transportation Department has launched a number of lawsuits against airlines because pilots had banned passengers they thought were security risks. In O'Sullivan's view, the department was more concerned that these exclusions may have been prompted partly by racial profiling than it was about the safety of passengers. The writer contends that the GOP's current internal struggles over the intelligence bill indicate that the United States will continue to treat homeland security as a displacement activity until the next time thousands of innocent people are murdered—and possibly even after that.

Mend It. *The New Republic*, v. 229 p9 October 13–20, 2003.

The editors of the *New Republic* argue that the USA PATRIOT Act may not be as important for fighting terrorism as the Bush administration insists nor as serious a threat to civil liberties as critics fear. In a recent report to Congress, the Justice Department conceded that it was increasingly using its new powers under the act to investigate crimes with no connection to terrorism. Moreover, in response to complaints from librarians concerned that they might be forced to release the records of innocent patrons, Attorney General John Ashcroft acknowledged that Section 215 of the act, allowing FBI agents to obtain any tangible item that they claim is related to an international terrorism investigation, had not been invoked once since the law was passed. However, the authors point out, instead of acknowledging critics' legitimate arguments, the administration is now trying to extend the reach of the PATRIOT Act.

Home Front. Jeffrey Rosen. *The New Republic*, v. 230 pp14–16 May 17, 2004.

According to the author, the Bush administration's detention of terrorist suspects is in many ways unprecedented. It has established a new category of detainees called "enemy combatants," suspects who may never be tried by the military or the civilian justice system and may be held indefinitely until the conclusion of a war on terrorism that might never end. If President Bush had asked the Republican Congress for assistance, Rosen claims, he would have secured an extensive law of preventive detention; instead, the administration opted to compound the dangers of preventive detention by making up its procedures as it went along. Preventive detention might be necessary, Rosen writes, but it cannot take place without meaningful oversight from independent organizations outside the executive branch.

Prevent Defense. Jeffrey Rosen. *The New Republic*, v. 231 pp16–18 September 6, 2004.

The Justice Department's terrorism-prevention plan involves prosecuting suspicious individuals quickly for low-level crimes, rather than waiting for years to build a stronger case. Rosen maintains that this is an ineffectual way of preventing larger atrocities from occurring. Although the increased sharing of information between law enforcement and intelligence officials has helped uncover terrorist plots, new prosecution policies have resulted in the prosecution or deportation of hundreds of people who have nothing to do with terrorism. As a result, Rosen claims, political support for the war on terrorism has been undermined in communities where support is crucial.

Terror & the Attack on Civil Liberties. Ronald Dworkin. *The New York Review of Books*, v. 50 pp37–41 November 6, 2003.

Dworkin claims that in its response to the terrorist threat, the Bush administration has ignored or violated many individual rights and liberties in a way that may change the character of the United States for the worse. The administration has vastly expanded both its surveillance of private individuals and its collection of data about them. It has also detained many hundreds of prisoners, some of them U.S. citizens, indefinitely, in secret, and without charge or access to a lawyer. There has been strong criticism of these policies by civil liberties groups, journalists, conservatives who worry about liberty, and others. The administration has, however, been remarkably successful in persuading federal judges to uphold its policies against legal challenge, and international lawyers are divided over whether the practices contravene any of the United States' treaty obligations.

From Afghanistan to Saudi Arabia, via Guantanamo. Joel Brinkley. *The New York Times*, pA4 October 16, 2004.

In an interview with Brinkley, Yaser E. Hamdi, a U.S. citizen and alleged "enemy noncombatant," discusses his experiences during and after his apprehension by U.S. troops in Afghanistan in 2001. For nearly three years Hamdi was detained at Guantanamo Bay, then placed in solitary confinement in Virginia and South Carolina military brigs until a Supreme Court decision found that he could no longer be detained without due process. In October 2004 a newly-freed Hamdi renounced his U.S. citizenship and returned to his ancestral home in Saudi Arabia.

Lesser Evils. Michael Ignatieff. *The New York Times Magazine*, pp46–51+ May 2, 2004.

According to Ignatieff, the chief ethical challenge of a war on terror is to protect the human rights of those who have violated the rights of U.S. citizens. Even terrorists are entitled to human rights, he argues, and the people of the United States must respect these rights because they are fighting a war whose essential goal is to protect the identity of democratic society and prevent it from becoming what terrorists believe it to be. Terrorists seek to provoke the United States into lawlessness in order to expose what they believe to be a core of treachery behind the country's promises of freedom. In response, the writer holds, the United States must demonstrate that the rule of law is not a mask or an illusion.

Subversive Reading. Margaret Talbot. *The New York Times Magazine*, p19–20 September 28, 2003.

Talbot discusses resistance measures that librarians have taken in response to the PATRIOT Act. The American Library Association and many of its members, indignant about a provision of the act that could force them to cooperate with federal agents by turning over the borrowing records of library patrons, have unleashed harsh criticisms of the government's approach to gathering information. Some librarians have reported that they are deliberately shredding records, whereas others remind patrons that if they return books on time, their records will be purged automatically.

We're Fighting Terror, But Killing Freedom. Randall Hamud. *Newsweek*, v. 142 p11 September 1, 2003.

The writer discusses his experiences as a lawyer defending Arabs and Muslims since September 11, 2001. In fighting terrorism, Hamud argues, the Bush administration is playing fast and loose with the rights of U.S. citizens. According to the author, the Constitution does not allow citizens arrested on U.S. soil to be held beyond the reach of the courts. Yet the PATRIOT Act allows federal agents to search homes and offices without the owners' knowledge, and force banks, doctors, and even libraries to turn over personal records.

The Road to the Brig. Michael Isikoff and Daniel Klaidman. *Newsweek*, v. 143 pp26+ April 26, 2004.

Isikoff and Klaidman discuss various perspectives on how U.S. citizens with suspected ties to Al Qaeda should be treated, a thorny issue since the terrorist attacks of September 11, 2001. While Attorney General John Ashcroft has argued consistently in favor of maintaining traditional systems of criminal justice, Vice President Dick Cheney and Defense Secretary Donald Rumsfeld have argued that accused persons should be sequestered in military brigs as "enemy combatants," with no right to trial or to see a lawyer. "Informal" rules have been set to determine whether a detained U.S. citizen should be thrown into the brig or brought to trial, but the Supreme Court will decide whether the president is allowed to lock up U.S. citizens suspected of terrorist links indefinitely, without charges. The Court will also hear a case to decide if foreign detainees at Guantanamo Bay have any legal rights.

Civil Liberties and Enemy Combatants. Harvey Silverglate. *Reason*, v. 36 pp22–29 January 2005.

According to Silverglate, the Supreme Court's widely praised June 28 rulings on "enemy combatants" are bad for the United States. Although many have interpreted the rulings as firm statements of judicial authority in the face of an executive abusing his own powers, the author argues that the reality is far less positive. In his view, widespread assertions about the triumph of liberty were premature and, in all likelihood, profoundly erroneous; each decision, he maintains, featured sufficient qualifications and concessions to undermine in practice the due-process rights that the justices lauded in theory.

Why We Need a Federal Marriage Amendment. Mathew D. Staver. *USA Today*, v. 133 pp56–57 September 2004.

Staver argues that the U.S. Constitution should be amended to protect traditional marriage between one man and one woman. In the writer's opinion, sanctioning same-sex marriage would destabilize the health, welfare, education, and morals of the United States and would eventually lead to the legalization of polygamy and polyamorousness. Marriage is not something with which people should experiment, he maintains, and it certainly is not amenable to having same-sex marriage in some states but not in others.

Law in a New Sort of War. Chitra Ragavan. *U.S. News & World Report*, v. 136 pp34–36 April 26, 2004.

Ragavan discusses the experiences of "enemy combatants" who are taking cases before the U.S. Supreme Court to plead for legal rights. At issue are the rights of some 650 alleged Taliban and Al Qaeda fighters detained incommunicado and without access to lawyers for two years at the U.S. Navy base at Guantanamo Bay and in a U.S. Navy brig in South Carolina. The Supreme Court will have to decide whether U.S. courts have jurisdiction to consider legal challenges to the detention of foreign nationals seized abroad and held at Guantanamo Bay. Specifically, the Court will study a March 2003 ruling by the U.S. Court of Appeals for the D.C. Circuit that stated that foreign nationals held outside the United States do not possess the "privilege of litigation" before U.S. courts.

A Time to Choose. Amy Sullivan. *The Washington Monthly*, v. 35 pp19–23 December 2003.

In October 2003, the Senate passed and President Bush signed the Partial-Birth Abortion Ban, thus enacting the first-ever federal ban of a specific abortion procedure. Anti-abortion activists celebrated the fact that the legislation, first introduced in Congress eight years ago and vetoed on two occasions by President Bill Clinton, was now law. Abortion-rights organizations were dispirited but unsurprised by their defeat and expected the legislation to be ruled unconstitutional; indeed, three federal judges have since made independent decisions blocking the ban. The writer examines the reasons why Democrats have started to lose the abortion debate, despite the fact that the majority of U.S. citizens support a woman's right to choose.

Two Out of Three Ain't Bad. Peter Berkowitz. *The Weekly Standard*, v. 9 pp17–18 July 19, 2004.

The writer discusses the Supreme Court's recent rulings on several enemy-combatant detention cases. In *Rasul v. Bush*, the Court ruled that non-citizen or alien enemy combatants who have not set foot in the United States and are imprisoned outside of the territorial jurisdiction of any federal court in the U.S. nevertheless have a right to challenge their detentions in any federal district court they wish. According to Berkowitz, the Court's rulings vindicated the core constitutional principle that there is no unreviewable executive power to imprison individuals. Now, the writer maintains, work must be done to achieve the correct balance between conducting war effectively and maintaining the rule of law scrupulously.

The Library Lie. Joseph Bottum. *The Weekly Standard*, v. 9 p7 January 26, 2004.

The writer discusses Section 215 of the USA PATRIOT Act, which alters the Foreign Intelligence Surveillance Act of 1978 by enabling the FBI to examine "tangible things" in a terrorism investigation. Initial rumors of the section's possible application to libraries started to spread in late 2002. In January 2003 the American Library Association passed a resolution calling the PATRIOT Act "a present danger to the constitutional rights and privacy rights of library users," a statement that was reaffirmed in July 2003 and January 2004. However, Bottum points out that Section 215 has never been invoked and does not even mention libraries; it is aimed at sources such as airline, hotel, and bank records.

Index